THE SPIRITUAL PHILOSOPHY

THE
SPIRITUAL PHILOSOPHY

AS AFFORDING

A KEY TO THE SOLUTION OF SOME OF THE PROBLEMS OF EVOLUTION

A SEQUEL TO "SOME THOUGHTS ON GOD"

BY

REV. J. GURNHILL, B.A.

EMMANUEL COLLEGE, CAMBRIDGE; MORAL SCIENCE PRIZEMAN

AUTHOR OF

"A COMPANION TO THE PSALTER," ETC.

WIPF & STOCK · Eugene, Oregon

Wipf and Stock Publishers
199 W 8th Ave, Suite 3
Eugene, OR 97401

The Spiritual Theology
As Affording a Key to the Solution of Some of the Problems of Evolution
By Gurnhill, J.
Softcover ISBN-13: 978-1-7252-9632-9
Hardcover ISBN-13: 978-1-7252-9634-3
eBook ISBN-13: 978-1-7252-9633-6
Publication date 1/4/2021
Previously published by Longmans, Green, and Co., 1914

This edition is a scanned facsimile of the original edition published in 1914.

To

My dear Wife and Sons

IN APPRECIATION

OF MUCH VALUABLE HELP

THIS VOLUME IS GRATEFULLY

INSCRIBED

PREFACE

DR. TENNANT, in one of his recent lectures on "The Aim and Scope of Philosophy of Religion," has well defined philosophy as an endeavour " to attain, by means of reflection upon the order of Nature, and upon the religious experience of mankind, to a satisfactory theory of the world, its origin, its destiny, and its meaning." If I should be asked what I understand by the Spiritual Philosophy, I could not give my answer in words more appropriate and true than those I have quoted.

In my book, "Some Thoughts on God," my object was to show that the Spiritual Philosophy, as taught by Christianity, and as contained in, or inferred from, the sacred books of the Old and New Testaments, is that which best enables us to understand the process of Evolution, both as to its origin, its method, and its end; and to unify and co-ordinate in one consistent harmonious system the many and various results, whether objective or subjective, which have been evolved. My object in the present work is to follow the same line of thought into further detail, and strengthen the position I took up by such additional arguments as a more careful examination and deeper insight might enable me to bring forward.

We are told that, at the present time, great uncertainty prevails as to what is to be the future trend of philosophic thought, and I fully agree with M. Bergson in thinking that the only philosophy which can stand the test of time and preserve its identity amid the kaleidoscopic changes of human speculation, is that which can take in "all that is given," and harmonize the results in one consistent whole.

As the days of Scholasticism have passed away, so now, too, religious dogma is challenged to stand on its defence. The theologian and Christian advocate can no longer rely on traditional prestige or privilege, but must be prepared to justify their faith at the bar of modern criticism and philosophy.

Doubtless the present is a time of great unsettlement in the world of speculative thought. It is not civilization or religion only that is at "the cross-roads"; philosophy is in the same position of uncertainty. Witness the sudden and unexpected recrudescence of that sheer materialism which characterized the latter half of last century. A philosophy of some kind we must and shall have. The great question is, of what kind is it to be? Shall it be animistic and spiritual, or shall it be materialistic and mechanical?

In the hope that the present volume may be found helpful in deciding this question, the Author commends it to the thoughtful consideration of his Readers.

J. G.

Feb. 21*st*, 1914.

TABLE OF CONTENTS

	PAGE
PREFACE	v

CHAPTER I

INTRODUCTORY REMARKS

The thesis—Psychology—Physiological psychology—The Materialist's solution of psychological problems—Is this solution satisfactory? 1

CHAPTER II

ULTIMATE REALITIES OF THE PHYSICAL UNIVERSE

Old notions need revision—Matter—Ether—Physical and psychical energy—The category and synthesis of energy—Energy monistic—Conclusions 7

CHAPTER III

EVOLUTION AND CHRISTIAN THEOLOGY

The concepts of Deity as suggested by Evolution and as formulated by Christian theology, not discrepant—The doctrine of the Trinity, that of a threefold activity, implying Transcendence, Immanence, and Inspiration 15

CHAPTER IV

SECTION A

DIAGRAM (1), PSYCHICAL EVOLUTION IN ANIMALS

Professor Bergson's theory of life—Man Nature's reversionary legatee—The line of further development, psychical and spiritual—Remarks on Prof. Romanes' Diagram—Intelligence—Directivity—Design 18

CONTENTS

CHAPTER IV—*continued*

SECTION B

DIAGRAM (2), PSYCHICAL AND SPIRITUAL DEVELOPMENT IN MAN

Explanation of same—Consciousness—Percept, Apperception, Concept—Conation—Column I.—Column II., Percept I.—Consciousness and Self-consciousness—The Ego and personality—Birth of the soul 28

CHAPTER V

DIAGRAM (2), PERCEPT II.—RELIGIOUS CONSCIOUSNESS

Natural phenomena suggest spiritual noumena—Nature the first teacher of religion—Causality, utility, and directivity—Beauty, unlimited expanse, and the infinite—The grand and terrible—The Idea of God—Dreams and the ghost theory . . . 46

CHAPTER VI

MORAL CONSCIOUSNESS

Diagram (2), Column II., Percept III.—Ethical distinctions—The problem of good and evil—Views of Kant, Wundt, and W. James—Antithesis and its relation to psychical and spiritual development—A note of congruity 55

CHAPTER VII

MORAL CONSCIOUSNESS—*continued*

Primary concept: Moral law—Secondary concepts: Duty, responsibility, sin, and penalty 65

CHAPTER VIII

THE INCARNATION AND SPIRITUAL CONSCIOUSNESS

Percept IV.—The Incarnation considered under a threefold aspect: (a) The *a priori* point of view—(b) As presented in the Gospel records—(c) As indicated by the claims which Jesus made for Himself 77

CHAPTER IX

SPIRITUAL CONSCIOUSNESS—*continued*

The truth of the Incarnation, as witnessed by the consciousness of Jesus—The standing Miracle of all time—The picture of Jesus—Who painted this picture?—Conclusions 98

CONTENTS

CHAPTER X

SPIRITUAL CONSCIOUSNESS—*continued*

Primary concept arising from the Incarnation—Love, the Norm of the highest life, displayed in the Atonement 107

CHAPTER XI

SPIRITUAL CONSCIOUSNESS—*continued*

Some secondary concepts arising from the percept of the Incarnation: (a) The Personality and Fatherhood of God—(b) The Brotherhood of man, and Christian Socialism 115

CHAPTER XII

PERCEPT V.—THE HOLY SPIRIT

Rival spiritualistic theories: (a) The Pluralistic—(b) The Monistic or Unitary—The Holy Spirit in the Old and New Testament Scriptures: (a) In the Old Testament—(b) In the New Testament—Primary concept: Holiness—Secondary concept: The dignity of the body 121

CHAPTER XIII

THE SURVIVAL OF MAN

I. The argument from faith in the Incarnation—II. The argument from Evolution—The place of death in Evolution—Two theories of cerebral function in relation to thought: (a) The Production theory—(b) The Transmission theory—The Pauline view—III. The argument from spiritual manifestations and psychical research 131

CHAPTER XIV

RECAPITULATION AND CONCLUSION . . . 148

APPENDIX

NOTE A. Good and Evil 155
NOTE B. Additional Note on Consciousness 158
NOTE C. Sin 161

DIAGRAM No. 1 . . . . Chap. IV. Sect. A
DIAGRAM No. 2 . . . . Chap. IV. Sect. B
INDEX 165

THE SPIRITUAL PHILOSOPHY

CHAPTER I

INTRODUCTORY REMARKS

The thesis—Psychology—Physiological psychology—The materialist's solution of psychological problems—Is this solution satisfactory?

THE thesis I am attempting to defend in this volume is, that the Cause which underlies and sustains the universe in general, and the system of evolution in particular, is not materialistic; that the only philosophy which can integrate and harmonize the varied objects of our experience in one consistent whole must be of the spiritual order. It is now generally admitted, I suppose, that evolution is the method which has been adopted by the Creator, and not that of special creations, for peopling the earth with ever-ascending forms of life. This is the theory of creation which no one now is found to dispute. And my object is first to present the theory, not in its abstract, but, if I may so say, in its concrete form, when clothed with the flesh and blood, the facts and phenomena of our actual knowledge and experience.

Secondly, I wish to show that, when thus presented, the spiritual philosophy enables us to interpret and understand the meaning of evolution as an intelligible, orderly progression, conducted along a definite line and for a definite end and purpose; and also to forecast with a high degree of probability what is the future in store for humanity when the ultimate goal has been reached.

Psychology

Psychology, according to Dr. McDougall, is "the positive science of the behaviour of living things." I would rather call it the science engaged in the investigation of the laws which govern the growth and development of the psychè in all vital organisms, whether animals or man. But what do we understand by this term "psychè"? What is the meaning we have come to attach to it?

Literally and etymologically, the word *psychè* denotes something which blows or breathes.[1] As such it corresponds to the Latin *anima* (whence *animal*), and from the earliest times was used to denote the life and spiritual principle in vital

---

[1] From the Greek word ψύχειν = *to breathe* or *blow*.

organisms as distinguished from the merely material element.

In the Greek philosophy the psychè was held to be the seat of the will, desires, and passions; and then, later, as the equivalent of the soul and mind in man, embracing even the reason, the understanding, and the emotions.

We gather, then, that by the psychè we are to understand the life bearing principle in all vital organisms and the originating centre or core of all vital activity.

It is the expression used to denote the principle or element of conscious life. And as biologists are now of opinion that all forms of life, except perhaps the very lowest, possess some degree of consciousness, so they are all endowed with a *psychè* of greater or less development. And it is this common possession which binds together all the products of vital evolution, and unites even the intellectual soul of man with the lowest form of conscious life.

In other words, even an elementary knowledge of biology teaches us that, whatever may have been the factor at work to produce the gradual evolution of vital organisms, the organism itself, viewed as a whole, is not a single homogeneous product, but one composed of two essentially different elements—the one material and physiological, the other non-material and psychical. Every upward step in the evolutionary process means the progress of each of these elements towards a higher degree of differentiation and perfection.

Moreover, their progress is *pari passu*. As the physiological structure, and especially of the motori-sensor nerves and brain-cortex becomes more complete, so does the *psychè* receive a corresponding increase in its range and faculty.

Physiological Psychology

The term *physiological psychology* has been given to the connection between these two elements of the vital organism, and I shall have occasion to refer to it again later on. Put in plain English, it simply means, that there is a close connection and interaction between the two constituent elements of every conscious vital organism.

This composite nature of the vital organism is one of the great outstanding facts of evolution. It is one, moreover, of immense significance both for the biologist and the psychologist. What is the relation between these two component elements which seem so intimate and mutually necessary that neither can exist without the other? Which is the cause and which the effect? Or is the relation not one of cause and effect at all, but one of correspondence and mutual co-operation for a common end? If so, we must look for some other cause to which both alike are attributable; and we must ask beside, What is that common end for which they both exist in union?

If we compare their union to co-partnership, we should like to know which is the predominant partner, and whether it is of such a nature that to dissolve it would be fatal to both.

Such are some of the questions which are suggested by this great fact of the combination of the physical and psychical elements in every vital organism of the animal kingdom.

The Materialist's Solution

The Materialist, indeed, has a rough-and-ready way of dealing with them. Mental and psychical activity is due to molecular changes in the brain. The brain secretes thought as the liver secretes bile. All animals, even including man, are nothing but automata. "And the essence of the automaton theory is that all the activities of men are explicable as purely material and mechanical sequences, without invoking the assistance of mind or consciousness, or anything but matter and energy working under their ordinary laws. Consciousness appears only as an inert accompaniment of material cerebral changes."[1]

Again, to quote the same authority, "The physico-chemical law dominates the universe. . . .

---

[1] "Modern Science, and the Illusions of Bergson," with commendatory preface by Sir E. Ray Lankester, pp. 168-184.

It denies the existence of any *spirit* breaking into mechanical law."[1]

CAN THIS SOLUTION BE ACCEPTED?

Such, in brief, is the attitude of the Materialist, and such the explanation he offers us of psychical phenomena. Those who are unable to accept them are invited to consider how these, and pertinent questions arising out of them, are dealt with by the Spiritual Philosophy in the subsequent chapters of this book.

[1] *Loc. cit.*, p. 193.

CHAPTER II

ULTIMATE REALITIES OF THE PHYSICAL UNIVERSE

Old notions need revision—Matter—Ether—Physical and psychical energy—The category and synthesis of energy—Energy monistic—Conclusions.

It will hardly be a matter for surprise to be told that some even of our modern views and theories of evolution and the physical phenomena of the universe require revision and restatement from time to time, as our knowledge and experience of them increase. The march of science to victory, as often as not, lies over the bodies of the slain.

Matter

Take, for example, the ideas of matter which formerly, and even up to our own day, prevailed amongst scientific men and philosophers.

The Atomic Theory

It used to be thought that matter was a substance composed of atoms, which, as the name denotes, were incapable of further subdivision. We are told now that such is not the case.

Recent discoveries, especially that of radium

and radio-active bodies, have shown us that this old idea of matter is no longer tenable. Atoms are themselves composite bodies, consisting of molecules. And these molecules again are composed of electrons, that is, minute charges of electricity. What the essential nature of these electrons may be we do not yet know.[1] All that seems certain about them is that they are not material in the usual sense of the word. And we may ask, in passing, if this most recent discovery of science be true, what becomes of Haeckel's theory of "atoms with souls"?

Ether

Or take again the substance, if that term be admissible, of ether, which Sir Oliver Lodge and others have been investigating, and about which they have such wonderful things to tell us.[2]

The writer of the chapter on "The Universe" in the *Harmsworth Popular Science* speaks of ether as the "universal medium, the womb and tomb of all things" (p. 643).

---

[1] Dr. H. S. Williams, in an interesting article on this subject, which appeared in *Harper's Magazine* for June, 1913, remarks that the electron seems to be responsible for all manifestations of energy, and is regarded by many physicists as the sole constituent of matter. "It seems well within bounds, therefore, to say that this immeasurably minute particle, which is far and away the smallest thing of which present-day science has any knowledge, is at the same time the most important thing in the universe."

[2] See "Some Thoughts on God," Sec. II. pp. 103-106.

The French scientist Gustave le Bon says ether is the mother of matter, and he compares the genesis and dissolution of matter to the formation and melting of icebergs in the ocean. "That ocean, universal and continuous, is the ether" (p. 642).

The Russian chemist Mendeleeff held that ether was a form of matter, and he even gave it a place in his table or list of elements. But this view is not now accepted. One thing may be safely said—that our knowledge of the ether is still in its infancy. Possibly, as last century was the age of steam and electricity, so this twentieth century may be the age of etheric investigation and discovery.

We cannot call the ether matter in the ordinary sense, yet without it as an all-pervading infinitely extended medium, we could have neither light nor electricity. And without electricity there would be no electrons, and without electrons no molecules, and without molecules no atoms, and without atoms no matter.

Where, then, are we to draw the line between the material and the non-material? It seems an impossible task, for the sufficient reason that no such line exists.

The material seems to run up insensibly into the immaterial, and finally loses itself in it. And we find ourselves compelled to calculate and assess the physical factors and products of evolution no longer in terms of matter but of energy.[1]

ULTIMATE REALITIES OF THE PHYSICAL UNIVERSE

And though the mystery which surrounds the ether is yet unsolved, and may possibly long remain so, we seem justified in regarding ether and energy as the two ultimate realities of the physical universe.

There are many forms of physical energy, such as, to mention only one or two of them, the attraction of gravitation, magnetism, electricity, and chemical affinity. All these have played, and will doubtless continue to play, a most important part in universal or cosmic and even in terrestrial evolution.

OTHER FORMS OF ENERGY BESIDE THE PHYSICAL AND MECHANICAL

But these forms of physical energy are by no means the only forms of which we have experience. There is vital energy, for example, which, in the course of its development, discloses an intelligence, which, in its earliest manifestations, hardly rises above reflex action, but in the course of its evolutionary progress takes the form of

---

[1] "The old division of the physical universe into matter and energy, which provided material for so much writing and so much angry controversy only a generation ago, breaks down. Matter becomes resolved into a mode or manifestation of energy."—" The Universe," p. 642, *Harmsworth Popular Science*.

consciousness, until it attains its highest value in the self-conscious personal soul of man.

Here, then, under the head of vital evolution, we have another kind of energy quite distinct from the physical and mechanical energy. But, while these two forms are essentially distinct, they are yet closely connected and correlated. Without the physical energy there could be no vital energy as we know it. The latter is, so to speak, superimposed on the former. If it were not for the force of gravitation, birds could not fly in the air, nor fishes swim in the sea, nor man walk on the earth. Without the action of chemical energy there could be no metabolism, no conversion of inorganic into organic matter, no manufacture of chlorophyll, without which animal life on the earth would be impossible.

But while dependent on physical energy, the vital energy is supreme to it. Not only is it able to make use of the physical energies, but even, if need be, to arrest and oppose their action. The mountain stream descends by the force of gravitation into the plain. But the miller turns it on to his wheel in the wooded glen below to grind his corn for the service of men. And all the while the eagle is wheeling in majestic flight above the mountain-top; and the Alpine climber, spurred on by ambition to reach the summit, is bringing to bear a psychic energy which, in spite of gravitation, enables him to accomplish his object. These are only isolated examples to show how psychic energy, while in a measure dependent on physical energy, is yet superior to it. My readers will have no difficulty in finding many others, for Nature abounds with them.

In short, we might compare the evolution of energy to a house of several stories, but each built upon, and rising above, the one below it. The man who lives in an upper story thinks and knows nothing of the foundations of the house buried deep in the ground below him; but remove or shake that foundation, and the whole structure will fall to the earth a shapeless mass of ruins.

The Category of Energy

What, then, are we to say about these two forms of energy—the physical and the psychical? We have seen that, while they are different and distinct in their nature, they are yet so closely interwoven and so mutually dependent that without the former the latter could not exist.

We conclude, then, first, that they must both fall into place under *one category*, which embraces and is the synthesis of all forms of energy.

We conclude, secondly, that, if we are justified in assuming the existence of a Prime Cause behind Evolution, that Cause must be *a monistic energy*, which contains in it the potency of all the energies of which, under the method of Evolution, we have knowledge and experience.[1]

And we conclude, thirdly, that since the cause cannot be less than the effect, if the evolutionary method of creation has produced the self-conscious personal spirit of man, then of the Prime Cause, the Panergete, we must predicate no less.

He too, like ourselves, must be a self-conscious personal Being. For the idea of such a Being emerging from an unconscious *materies* is, to my mind at least, unthinkable. Behind that *materies*, within it and above it, there must be the self-conscious personal Mind, immanent in Nature, yet in its essence transcending Nature.

Let me close this chapter with the following significant utterance by Sir Oliver Lodge, in his recent book " Modern Problems " :—

" There are facts which suggest that there is a higher kind of existence—an existence already attained by our loftiest work, an existence

---

[1] To this energy the Greeks gave the name of *Panergete,* which means the All-effecting One. The classic passage is from the "Agamemnon" of Æschylus, and runs as follows:—

ἰώ, ἰή, διαί Διός
παναιτίου, πανεργέτα
τί γὰρ βροτοῖς ἄνευ Διός
τελεῖται;

which I venture thus to translate—

"Io, Ie, through mighty Zeus,—
The Panergete, the Cause of all.
For what to mortal men befalls,
Apart from Zeus?"

appropriate to creations of genius, a kind of existence or subsistence, or supersistence, which transcends present limitations, which has been raised or put ashore out of the current of the time-stream into a freer and diviner air, where the past, the present, and the future are united in the transcendental coexistence of a more copious reality."[1]

Our task in the next and following chapters will be to trace the gradual development of the psychic element in vital Evolution, and also to indicate the factors by which it has been secured in accordance with the principles and teaching of the Spiritual Philosophy.

[1] See also his Address to the students of Bedford University, January, 1914.

CHAPTER III

EVOLUTION AND CHRISTIAN THEOLOGY

The concepts of Deity, as suggested by Evolution and as formulated by Christian theology, not discrepant—The doctrine of the Trinity, that of a threefold activity, implying Transcendence, Immanence, and Inspiration.

My object in the last chapter was to show that the ultimate reality which underlies all phenomena, whether physical or mental or spiritual, is energy; that all forms of force and activity may be subsumed under the one category of energy; and that, if we are justified in assuming a Prime Cause of the evolutionary process, that Cause must be the synthesis of at least all the forms of energy of which we have any knowledge or experience.

And, in order to designate this all-comprehending monistic energy, I ventured to coin a new word, or rather to borrow an old one; namely, the *Panergete*, or All-effecting One. The word is used to denote the Supreme Being, Who is at once transcendent and omnipotent, God Almighty. But it differs somewhat in meaning from the latter designation of omnipotence, and brings rather into prominence the activity of God as manifesting

Himself by the exercise of His power. For as He is the synthesis and complexion of all energy, its Centre and its Source, so every form of energy, whether physical, psychical, or spiritual, is a partial manifestation of the infinite all-effecting Panergete in terms of the finite.

But here another question presents itself and demands an answer: Can this doctrine of the Supreme Being, as an infinite monistic energy, be brought into harmony with that of the Spiritual Philosophy as expressed in the language of Christian theology? The difficulty of reconciling the two will, I think, not be found so great as at first sight might appear. For what is the cardinal doctrine of that theology? We may define it in one single word. It is that of the Trinity. By which we understand:

1. The transcendence of a Divine Being, Who is the Source and Centre of all existence and energy; and Who for this reason is spoken of as the Father.

2. A second Person of one substance or Divine essence with the Father; Who, as drawing His existence (begotten) from the Father alone, is fitly called His Son; and Who, by virtue of the Divine energy is at once the Creator of the universe and immanent in it. As such He is also spoken of as the Logos, or Word of the Father, because He is the expression and executant of His will.

3. A third Person, proceeding from both the Father and the Son, and therefore sharing the attributes of both, their Divine energy and personality. In the Old Testament He is known as the Spirit of Divine Wisdom, the *Hokmah*, "sweetly ordering all things," the Giver of life, and the Source of wisdom and inspiration. In the New Testament He is called the *Paraclete*, a Divine spiritual energy of the highest character, inspiring, instructing, and sanctifying the souls of men.

Such, in brief, is the nature of the Deity, as held and taught by the Christian theologian. And it will hardly be denied, I think, that this view is strictly analogous to that which a study of the facts of our experience leads us to entertain.

The Father is the Source and Centre of all energy. The Son represents the active exercise of that energy. The Holy Ghost, its influence as the Source of wisdom and sanctification.[1]

[1] "The followers of Jesus were conscious of three ways in which they knew God. They were conscious of the working in them of a power to which they gave the name of the Holy Spirit, as they were conscious of the influence on them of Jesus Himself as Divine. And yet there was only one God—one Cause, one Principle, one Mind, one Will, one Life."—" Ethical Significance of Christian Doctrines," J. F. Bethune-Baker, D.D., *Cambridge Theological Essays*, p. 563. And again, "The experience and the teaching of Jesus, renewed in the consciousness of Christians, generation after generation, required the recognition of a threefold activity (energy)—a threefold mode of existence—within the Godhead itself."—*Ibid.*, p. 564.

CHAPTER IV

Section A

PSYCHICAL EVOLUTION IN ANIMALS

Professor Bergson's theory of life—Man Nature's reversionary legatee—The line of further development, psychical and spiritual—Prof. Romanes' Diagram, and remarks thereon—Intelligence—Directivity—Design.

WHAT is the true line of continuous development in the evolutionary process? Life has been compared by Bergson to an impulse or impetus striving to expand in any and every direction. To this expansive energy are attributed the infinite forms of life which people the earth. But geology teaches us plainly enough that the vital energy has not been successful in making its way at all times and in every direction against the downward tendency of matter and the force of opposing circumstances and conditions of life. The pathway of evolution is strewn all along with wrecks and failures, with forms of life which have flourished for a time, and then disappeared for ever.

In man, and man only, according to Bergson, has the vital energy been able to force its way through the opposing and depressing influence of matter, and continue on its upward course of evolution to the attainment of higher values.

Assuming that Bergson's theory is correct, then, of course, it would be vain to look for higher forms of animal life on the earth. The mere presence of man there, and the influence he is constantly exercising, often under the specious name of civilization, which is sometimes, alas! only another name for barbarism,[1] would render such further evolution improbable.

It may be so. But whether true or not—and we need not now discuss the question—we are still face to face with the problem of vital evolution in the case of man, where it is admitted neither to have failed nor yet to have reached its climax and completion. Here, at any rate, the process is still believed to be in progress. Man holds the field. He has taken possession of the earth. He is Nature's reversionary legatee, the heir of all the ages. Of all the organisms which ever have or still do share the vital impulse with him, there is not one which can long contest the supremacy with him, or say him "Nay." His charter of birthright still holds good, whenever or by whomsoever it was given him: "And you, be ye fruitful, and replenish the earth, and subdue it" (Gen. i. 28).

If evolution is one continuous act of becoming;

[1] I allude more particularly to the fiendish horrors which accompany seal-fishing, and the wholesale destruction of humming-birds and birds of paradise, etc., for the adornment of fashionable ladies' hats.

if life is the energetic principle which stands for progress, for development, for freedom; and if only in the life of man—the human race—is that principle still active, what we have a right to ask is, "What is the goal for which he is making, and what is the road by which he is ultimately to reach it?"

The Line of Further Progress Psychical

The question is indeed a real and momentous one. It is one, moreover, which I think we can only answer by taking into account the possibilities implied in the complex nature and varied content of human life.

Regarded physically, man is only an animal, and connected by descent with animals which share his physical nature, though occupying a position far lower in the scale of life than his own. It is true that, in some respects, though by no means in all, he has outstripped all his ancestral relatives. In the variety and delicacy of some of his sense perceptions, in his power of adaptation to different conditions of life, in reason and intelligence, he stands pre-eminent above them all. But these physical endowments and mental faculties, as they do not exhaust the content of his life, so neither are they the qualities and attributes which serve to distinguish him most clearly from all other forms of animal life.

If mental and psychic evolution had been

arrested at the point to which Romanes had traced it, and where he left it, then there would have been little or no foundation on which to build up a belief in the continued evolution of the human race, and the attainment by man, as an individual, of a higher and nobler form of existence. No foundation, I mean, as supplied by the psychic and spiritual content of his natural life. But it is not so. Man is, indeed, an animal. But in his case evolution has not been content to leave him merely such.

And if as philosophers we must seek to give him his rightful place in the scale of life, and forecast the possibilities or probabilities which still await him, then we are bound in reason to take into account those higher psychic and spiritual faculties of which, through the continued progress of evolution, he has become possessed, and by which there has been opened out for him a new chapter in the book of life.

"Philosophy," as Dr. Alfred Caldecott truly observes in his Cambridge Essay on "The Being of God" (p. 104), "is concerned to have before it human nature in its whole length, and breadth, and depth, and height. It must, moreover, take man as a living person, and decline every invitation to limit its view to any one elemental feature of his life."

This means, that if we would learn what man is, and gain some insight into his possible future, we must follow him in his evolutionary progress through the physical into the higher region of his psychical and spiritual development. For it is in this region only, so it seems, that his further evolution is to be carried on. And it is here alone we shall perceive the destiny which may yet be in store for him; namely, in the affinity and union of his personal soul with the Parent Spirit of God. Nor let us suppose that there is here in this progress any breach of continuity. For it is one and the same Source and Giver of life, to Whom he owes his being, Who is henceforth by further and fuller manifestations and outpourings of His Spirit to lead him onwards and upwards to perfect union and fellowship with Himself.

But in saying this, I am conscious I am giving utterance to a proposition, or perhaps a series of propositions, which I have no right to assume will be accepted without further demonstration.

I shall, therefore, crave both the patient attention and generous indulgence of my reader, while I endeavour to show (1) how far Prof. Romanes brought us by his study and analysis of "Mental Evolution in Animals," and (2) to ascertain what further steps in intellectual and psychical development have since been taken to bring the human race up to the point of its present psychical and spiritual attainment.

Mental Evolution in Animals

In his very interesting book on "Mental Evolution in Animals," the late Prof. Romanes has indicated the successive steps whereby he conceived the evolutionary process had been carried forward up to that point to which it was his purpose to trace it.

But that purpose was strictly limited. The scope of his inquiry was confined to the investigation of the growth of mentality, that is, of intelligence, conscious or unconscious, in the animal world. It is true it embraces man; but it is man only as the highest form or example of animal life. And the further evolution of man in his psychical and spiritual nature did not at that time come within the range of his inquiry. That he would have done this also, had he lived, I cannot entertain a doubt. And we must ever regret that his premature death probably deprived the world of what would have been a priceless contribution alike to science, to philosophy, and religion.

Prof. Romanes happily has drawn out a table or diagram giving us a bird's-eye view of the principal results of his inquiry.

Prof. Romanes' Diagram

This diagram I have reproduced, in a somewhat abbreviated form, for a double purpose; first, because it gives us a synopsis of psychical evolution in the animal kingdom up to, but not including man; secondly, because I think it will form an excellent starting-point for the further consideration of the higher psychical development in man himself—the process whereby the animal *psychè* has been transformed into the personal self-conscious spirit ($\pi\nu\epsilon\hat{\upsilon}\mu\alpha$) or *soul* of man.

Referring to Romanes' diagram, the reader will observe that, starting from the earliest form of vital activity known to us, namely, protoplasm, he traces the growth of evolution upwards through neurility and nervous sensibility to reflex action and volition (will).

This line of development represents, according to Romanes, the main channel or current of vital evolution. But, from it, side-currents are given off on either hand: the one on the right represents the line of intellectual or mental development; that on the left, the line of emotional and psychical development. For a full explanation of the diagram, however, I must refer my readers to Romanes' work itself, chap. v.

Design and Intelligence in Vital Evolution

The book has yet to be written showing the many and various ways in which the Divine wisdom, the Hokmah of the Wisdom writers, has been manifested in vital evolution. But some of these ways stand out with a prominence which can scarcely fail to carry conviction. For my present purpose it will suffice if I mention only two or three of them.

(1) Take, for example, the marvellous skill and wisdom displayed in the physiological structure of plants and animals, and in the adoption and adaptation of means to an end. So marvellous are they, indeed, so amazing in their delicacy, their beauty and arrangement, that were they not matters of fact and observation, we should pronounce them incredible and inconceivable.

(2) Take again the subject of instinct, which is the common characteristic of vital evolution both in plants and animals, and by which appropriate actions are performed, apparently without any conscious intelligence or purpose of the organism itself, as for instance the instincts of self-preservation and reproduction with their corresponding appetites, passions, and emotions, hunger and thirst, love and hatred, anger and revenge.

There are those who would persuade us that utility is the one sole motive and purpose, so to speak, of all vital evolution, the fundamental law of what is called natural selection. It seems plausible enough, but such a theory utterly breaks down in the manifest presence in Nature of a power which works for beauty as perfectly distinct from utility.

(3) Or take again the subject of mimicry, which, in spite of the attempt to explain it on the utilitarian theory of natural selection, is thought

by many to point to an intelligence, working for a purpose, indeed, but without any conscious co-operation on the part of the organism itself.

As for the display of conscious intelligence as distinct from instinct, it is so common as hardly to need mention.

Now, all these are manifestations of the Intelligence which underlies and energizes the whole process of vital evolution in the animal world. What shall we say of it? Is it all mere mind-stuff, a sort of free intelligence into which the element of conscious personality does not enter? At first sight it might appear so, because no personality emerges. But a more careful consideration will show us, I think, that such is not the case. For, whatever else we may say about these manifestations, there are two features about them which cannot be denied. They disclose *purpose* and the use and adaptation of means to an end; and secondly, they disclose *directivity*. But what do purpose and directivity denote? Surely nothing less than a self-conscious Personal Spirit, immanent in nature, yet transcending nature, the Hokmah, or Spirit of Divine wisdom, which " sweetly ordereth all things." [1]

[1] "If we adopt the 'physical and physiological account' as the whole truth, proclaiming ourselves materialists and declaring man to be merely '70 kilogrammes of material,' moved by physical and chemical forces, we find ourselves hopelessly unable to explain purposeful and intelligent behaviour. Our theory breaks down just when it is required to explain what is obviously the most characteristic attribute of man. So clear is this that, if we think it necessary to

In presence of the facts of psychical evolution in animals, as indicated in Prof. Romanes' diagram, materialism is unable to offer any explanation which can satisfy the reasonable and logical demands of the human mind. And the only system which can do so, I submit, is that of the Spiritual Philosophy.

In the next chapter I shall endeavour to show how by continuation of the same process of evolution and by the activity and influence of the same Divine energies to which we have given the names of the Logos and the Hokmah—Word and the life-giving Spirit of wisdom—the animal psychè has become transformed into self-conscious personal soul of man.

choose between the two opposed views, we shall end by accepting the view of psychology and of every day."—*Harmsworth Popular Science,* pt. 30, p. 3584.

CHAPTER IV—*continued*

SECTION B

PSYCHICAL AND SPIRITUAL DEVELOPMENT IN MAN

Diagram No. 2—Explanation of same—Consciousness—Percept, apperception, concept—Conation—Column I.—Column II., Percept I.—Consciousness and self-consciousness—The Ego and personality—Birth of the soul.

PERHAPS I shall best serve my purpose, indicated at the close of the last chapter, by following the example of Prof. Romanes, and giving in the form of a diagram a sort of a bird's-eye view of the method and the means which seem to have been employed, in accordance with the principles of Spiritual Philosophy, for the psychical development of the human race.

EXPLANATORY REMARKS

The diagram speaks for itself. Nevertheless, a few explanatory remarks will probably assist the reader to understand it; though no amount of explanation on my part will obviate the need for thoughtful study on his, if he wishes to do so. He will observe that the subject-matter is arranged in four columns.

Column I. contains a brief statement of the radical causes to which, according to the view of the Spiritual Philosophy, the whole process of evolution is due: namely, increasing manifestations of the Logos or Word, and the Hokmah or Holy Spirit : A, in the natural and physical sphere ; B, in the supernatural and spiritual.

Column II. contains a brief summary, by no means exhaustive, of our principal percepts ; that is, things perceived and experienced by us, whether by our bodily senses or our mental and spiritual faculties.

Column III. indicates the concepts, primary and secondary, to which the percepts by apperception give rise.

Column IV. represents the successive psychical increments and enrichments of the personal soul, due to higher moral and spiritual concepts. These increments, it will be observed, are expressed in terms of growing consciousness. Consciousness as exhibited by anthropoid apes was the highest point of psychical development reached in Romanes' diagram. It is also the starting-point which marks the commencement of the upward progress of the human psychè, through self-consciousness to religious, moral, and finally to spiritual consciousness.

For the purpose of easier reference, I have numbered and lettered the different percepts, or classes of percepts, in column II., with their corresponding consequents in columns III. and IV.

It must not be supposed, however, for a moment that the list of percepts, or classes of percepts, is set out as complete and exhaustive. Far from it. Doubtless there are many others, beside those specified, which have given rise to their corresponding concepts, and so enriched the psychic consciousness. I have only specified those which seemed to be more important, and to have exercised a greater influence in this respect.

We now come to what is contained within the dark enclosing line, and as my object at present is to indicate what I conceive to be the method whereby vital evolution has been, and is being, carried forward in the human species beyond the highest point of mental development attained in animal life, as commonly understood, I have been content to accept without criticism the conclusions of Prof. Romanes as summarized in his Diagram of Mental Evolution in Animals.[1]

Consciousness

Consciousness, then, is adopted as our starting-point. It is fitting that it should be so, because from this point the psychical history of man as distinguished from the rest of the animal world begins. The difference between consciousness and self-consciousness is just that discrimen or distinction which separates the highest form of

---

[1] A digest or abstract of this diagram will be found facing Chap. IV., Sect. A.

intelligence reached by, say, the anthropoid apes and man. They are conscious, but, as we believe, not self-conscious. Man is not only conscious, but self-conscious.

Consciousness, indeed, is the common attribute or characteristic of all life. But in man it becomes the core or nucleus, so to speak, around which have been collected and crystallized the successive increments of intellectual and psychical value which have made man what we know him to be, the very highest product of vital evolution.

How vast the difference between an amœba and a man! Yet both are links in the unbroken chain of life. And consciousness is the common property which bridges over the gulf between the two, and makes them both akin; the point of difference being the content of their consciousness.

We next come to what I would describe as the mechanism of the system whereby the evolutionary process is carried forward in the higher range of human life, and whereby the conscious animal psychè is gradually developed into the personal self-conscious soul of man.

Percept, Apperception, Concept

Percepts by apperception give rise to, or are transmuted into, concepts; and concepts, as they arise and are assimilated by the mind, expand and enrich the consciousness. But these terms Percept, Apperception, and Concept represent factors or functions which have a very important part to play in the development of human consciousness. It is essential, therefore, that their meaning and the sense in which they are used should be clearly apprehended.

Percepts [1]

Perception (*per capio*) we define as the taking in through the senses of the body, or the cognitive faculties of the mind, impressions of objects external to the perceiving agent or subject. Thus all things of which we can form any idea, all things cognizable by us, may be subsumed under two heads or categories—the Ego, which is the perceiving conscious self; and the Non-Ego, which stands for the things perceived.

The term Percept, then, is capable of a double meaning. First, *objective*, as denoting the object perceived; second, subjective, as denoting the picture or impression formed, say, on the retina of the eye, or the tympanum of the ear, and then by means of nerve structures conveyed to the sensorium of the brain, which we may call the receiving house of the conscious mind. And, generally speaking, the conscious psychical Ego of man may fitly and truly be compared to a mirror held up to Nature, which reflects the objects of

---

[1] " Perception is solely of the *here* and *now :* Conception is of the like and unlike, of the future, of the past, of the far away."—Prof. W. James, " Some Problems of Philosophy," pp. 74 and 108.

the non-ego, or outer world; perhaps, even still more correctly, to the sensitized plate or film of the photographer, which not only receives the image or picture to which it is exposed, but fixes and reproduces it in a permanent form.

But while external, and for the most part material phenomena are the cause in the first instance of our mental percepts, it behoves us to be on our guard against the errors into which the materialistic philosophers—even Descartes and Huxley—of the last century fell. According to them, all mental and psychical activity was to be explained and accounted for on purely materialistic and mechanical principles. There was no such thing as free will, and man himself became a mere automaton.

WHAT IS THE SUBJECT-MATTER OF OUR PERCEPTS?

What, then, are our percepts?—I mean the external objects of which, by the senses of the body or the faculties of the mind, we become conscious? Shall we say they are anything else than the various phenomena which form our environment, and which, in accordance with the spiritual philosophy, we attribute to the Divine energies of the creative Logos and the life-giving Spirit? Are they not the lesson-book, which the All-Father has put into the hands of His children to teach them about Himself and fit them for union and communion with Him?

APPERCEPTION

It hardly needs to be said that apperception is a form of mental activity, somewhat analogous to the function of digestion and assimilation in the body. As by the latter function food is converted into bodily tissue, so by the former, percepts, which are impressions or pictures received from the outer world, are by a sort of process of mental digestion transmuted into psychical concepts, which help to build up the spiritual edifice of the soul or self-conscious Ego.

"The process of apperceptive synthesis," says Dr. McDougall, "produces a simplification of the structure of the mind, and of the language which reflects it, by which they are rendered more effective instruments of thinking.

"The classical instance of original apperception usually cited is Newton's discovery of the likeness between the motion of the moon and that of falling bodies, and his consequent thinking of all such processes as examples of gravitation."[1]

According to Kant, "Apperception is a word used to signify that when a new perception is acquired, it is not merely added to, but is fused into harmony with, the already existing furniture of the mind."

It means the power to translate percepts into concepts, and add them to the content of the

[1] "Psychology," pp. 92 ff.

already existing consciousness of the human mind.

Kant, in his "Critique of Pure Reason," tells us that the process of knowledge depends in the first instance on two factors: first, the senses as the organs by which percepts of external phenomena are conveyed to the mind; and secondly, the understanding, by which they are, so to speak, digested, thought out, and so assimilated and added to the psychical consciousness.

Phenomena, in short, by this process are translated into *noumena*.[1]

Prof. Reid understands by the term, "That degree of perception which reflects as it were upon itself; by which we are conscious of our existence, and conscious of our own perceptions. Similarly, Leibniz defines it as the faculty whereby the percipient becomes conscious of a perception.

Generally speaking, then, the function of apperception is to convert or transform or translate percepts into concepts.[2]

The percept of consciousness as an objective fact, either in myself or any other creature, begets the *idea* of consciousness in the abstract; and this concept, considered in relation to myself, produces self-consciousness. The intelligent reasoning psychè becomes by apperception a

---

[1] *Cf.* Rom. i. 20.
[2] In Murray's "English Dictionary," apperception is defined as "the mind's perception of itself as a conscious agent."

self-conscious personality. The soul is born, and can say for the first time, "I am conscious of my own consciousness."

It is that faculty which, perhaps more than any other, forms the distinctive characteristic of mankind.

It marks the turning-point in psychic development. Animals have perception, but not apperception. Consequently their psychic consciousness remains fixed at the same level, while to that of man a future of boundless expansion and elevation is open.

We might compare it not inaptly to the lever whereby man is enabled to raise himself higher and higher in the scale of psychic evolution.

Concepts [1]

Our concepts are the result of the effort of the mind to idealize the percepts which are submitted to it from the outer world.

Our percepts are, for the most part, physical and phenomenal; our concepts, on the other hand, are metaphysical and noumenal. And as our percepts, objectively considered, form our

---

[1] "Concepts are just as real in their 'eternal' way as percepts are in their temporal way. What is it to be real? The best definition I know is that which the pragmatic rule gives. Anything is real of which we find ourselves obliged to take account in any way. Concepts are thus as real as percepts; for we cannot live a moment without taking account of them."—"Some Problems of Philosophy," p. 101, by Prof. W. James.

CONCEPTS AND CONATION 37

environment, so our concepts may be regarded as the response to that environment. Each addition to the sum of our percepts ought, if there be a proper response, to result in a corresponding increment to the sum of our concepts, that is, of our psychical equipment.

Thus, for example, beautiful objects beget the idea or concept of the beautiful, as something which gives us pleasure, something to be admired, and therefore loved and sought after. But every form of beauty is but a concrete expression of the beautiful as an attribute of the transcendent Mind or Soul of the universe, Whom we call God.

Thus, concepts are the efforts of the self-conscious personal soul of man to idealize the reality which underlies the phenomenal percepts; for reality in some of its forms does underlie all percepts, which are only manifestations of the Infinite Mind in terms of the finite. And the function of the human mind is to gather up finite percepts and transmute them into ideal concepts as constituent elements of the one great Reality, *the Idea of God.*

CONATION

There is yet one other element or factor required to complete the full cycle of psychical activity and progress. It is what Dr. McDougall calls conation, *i.e.* effort or affective disposition. These are his words: "The primitive cycle of purposive or mental activity seems to be cognition, evoking feeling and conation, which conation, issuing in bodily activity, brings about a new cognition that in turn brings a feeling of satisfaction and terminates the conation."[1]

It is not enough to have percepts, nor yet the concepts to which by apperception they give rise; there must, in addition, be the conative response to the concept, so as to make it a rule of conduct for the formation and elevation of character.

Column I.

If the reader will now turn to column I. of the diagram, he will observe that all the percepts fall under two heads or categories—

A. Physical and natural.

B. Metaphysical and spiritual.

The percepts which fall under each of these heads may appear at first sight to be heterogeneous. But, according to the teaching of the spiritual philosophy, all percepts and phenomena, both physical and spiritual, are due to one and the same efficient Cause, namely, the Divine energy present in the universe by virtue of the creative Logos and the life-giving Spirit. Even the Incarnation itself, and the gift of the Paraclete Spirit, are of the same order, and differ only from

---

[1] "Psychology," p. 105. Though I have not made use of the terms "cognition" and "conation," the reader will readily perceive that they are involved in the terms "percept" and "response to environment."

previous percepts in being more direct and personal manifestations of the same Divine Agencies.

But not only are all our percepts, both natural and revealed, connected by identity of origin and efficient cause, they are so also by similarity of method and unity of purpose. For all our percepts fall under the head of evolution. And the final purpose and end of evolution, as far as we can judge, seem to be the production of individual souls capable of union and communion with the Fount of all consciousness, the Parent Spirit of God.[1]

Having now explained the meaning and use of the terms *Percept, Apperception, Concept,* and *Conation,* which play such a prominent part in the psychical development of man, I shall now invite my reader's attention to some of those specific examples of the transformation of percept into concept which are to be found in the diagram.

[1] The following extract from Prof. Bergson's article on "Life and Consciousness" is much to the point:—" May we not, therefore, suppose that the passage of consciousness through matter is destined to bring to precision—in the form of distinct personalities—tendencies or potentialities which at first were mingled, and also to permit these personalities to test their force, whilst at the same time measuring it by an effort of self-creation . . . and are we not led to suppose that the effort continues beyond . . . preparing them, by the very effort which each of them is called to make, for a higher form of existence?"
—*Hibbert Journal,* October, 1911, p. 43. I hardly need point out the correspondence between Bergson's view as to the end and object of the evolutionary process and that suggested in the text.

Column II.—Percept I.

CONSCIOUSNESS, AND ITS TRANSFORMATION INTO SELF-CONSCIOUSNESS

This must have been the first step in the upward progress whereby primitive man became differentiated from his nearest ancestral relatives in the animal kingdom—assuming, of course, the uniform working of the evolutionary system in regard to man.

Previous to that step a high degree of intelligent and psychic development had already been attained. There was consciousness, but no self-consciousness. There was selfness, or, as the Germans express it, *Selbst-heit*, expressing itself chiefly through the instinct of self-preservation. But self-consciousness proper first began to appear when the intelligent animal psychè turned its thought, by a kind of mental reflex action, inward upon itself, and so became the subject of its own consciousness.

This act, which seemed so simple, was indeed one of the highest import for the future of the human race. It was the very starting-point of the new chapter in psychical evolution. It denoted nothing less than the birth of the Ego, or soul as a free and independent personality; a being who for the first time was able to utter those two brief words so full of significance, "*I am*," and "I am because I can think "—*Cogito ergo sum.* We have egoism and existence combined in one self-conscious personal being.

Free Will

Nor was this all. There had been "will" before the birth of the self-conscious soul. But that will had been restricted to very narrow limits. It had been little more, in fact, than the expression of the instinct of self-preservation. But with the birth of self-consciousness the soul of man attained—not perfect freedom, indeed, but freedom of a far higher order and wider range. The self-conscious Ego that could say, "I am because I can think," could also say, "I am free because I am no longer bound down by the restraints of instinct and mere self-preservation as the only law of my psychical activity, but free to act as reason and deliberation may suggest." Thus by apperception the conscious psychè became transformed into the personal Ego, and concurrently with this transformation the Ego obtained its franchise as a free agent.

The Ego and Personality

The following remarks of Professor Wundt on this subject are so apposite that I need not apologize for quoting them :—

"The Ego's self-discrimination is involved in its

inner and outer acts of will, and it is in the direct perception of his own activity that the individual discovers himself as a separate personality . . . For out of the multitude of actions performed by an individual, it is the inner acts, *the acts of apperception*, that stand out as more original and immediate than the rest; while the outward movements, important though they may be for the earliest stages of self-discrimination, represent merely the consequences of particular kinds of apperceptions. Hence the final stage in this development consists in the individual's discovery that his own innermost being is pure apperception; that is, an inner voluntary activity distinguished from the rest of conscious content. The Ego feels itself to be the same at every moment of its life, because it conceives the activity of apperception as perfectly constant, homogeneous in its nature, and coherent in time . . . As the Ego is the will in its distinction from the rest of conscious content, so personality is the Ego reunited to the manifold of this content, and thereby raised to the stage of self-consciousness."[1]

Birth of the Soul

If we were asked to suggest a time when man became a living soul, through the inspiration of

[1] Prof. Wundt, "Principles of Morality," pp. 20, 21.

the Spirit (Breath) of God, described in the anthropomorphic language of Gen. ii. 7, we should say without hesitation it was when that mighty evolution took place which transformed the conscious animal psychè into the personal self-conscious Ego of man. To use a simple illustration, it was as though the great Artificer had inserted an Æolian harp in the soul of man, capable of responding to airs Divine. Great as was the change in itself, it was greater still because it prepared the way for subsequent psychic developments in consciousness, which otherwise could never have taken place, and by which the human soul has come to be what it is.[1]

That a change so great, so significant in the

[1] The following extracts from Prof. Wundt's "Principles of Morality" are quite germane to the subject under discussion, and I commend them to the consideration of the thoughtful reader :—

"As the various psychical activities of thought, feeling, and will are distinguishable only by a process of abstraction, and are themselves inseparable elements of conscious life, so the idea of a soul distinct from the content of consciousness is nothing but the empty concept of the unity and constant coherence of psychical activities, hypostatized into a real substance" (p. 32).

"Thus the individual is simply the last member of a series whose ascending order is lost in infinity. Hence religion postulates to complete this infinite *regressus*, the Divine will as the last and highest unity out of which develop all the stages of the finite realization of will." "Religion associates the idea of God with that of a guiding Spirit, Whose personal volition is the ultimate ground of all psychical development. . . . In the idea of a transcendent Deity religious thought thus combines the two elements of will which are for ever separated in the phenomenal world. For to the religious consciousness God is the creative World-Will, which means that He is at once individual and social Will" (pp. 36, 37).

psychical evolution of man was also attended by some corresponding change in the physiological structure of the brain as the physical organ of thought and mentality, we may not doubt. But this is an aspect of the question which does not fall within the scope of this inquiry. Those of my readers who may wish to follow it up, I would recommend to read a very interesting and suggestive article on "Man" in the *Harmsworth Popular Science*, Pt. 32, pp. 3830–3832.[1]

One word more. At any and every point in the history of psychological development, the human soul is the sum-total of its psychical endowments and activities at that point. From which it follows, that if the latter are capable of

---

[1] The following brief extracts will suffice to show the nature and drift of the article:—

"There is every reason to believe that the specially characteristic parts of the mind of man, the intelligence and the ego, or self, must have their seat in just that portion or those connected portions of the brain which Haeckel calls the *phronema*, and that the pre-frontal area, which we find to be the newest and most characteristic feature of the modern brain, comprises, at any rate, a very great and essential part of this *phronema*—the organ of the central part of the mind."

"It is the *phronema* that makes man man; it is even, we see, the *phronema* that makes modern man what he is as compared with the indisputably human creatures of the Neanderthal race and its predecessors." "It is the centre of will, and of self-control, it is the centre of attention, or of what Wundt calls 'apperception.'"

"This core or centre, this intensely conscious, because self-conscious, nucleus of the personality (the ego, or soul) is the unique characteristic of the psychè of man, and places him even a world apart from the highest of the higher animals."

further increase, as the Spiritual Philosophy justifies us in believing, and exactly in proportion as they do increase, the soul will continue its upward and endless progress of approximation and resemblance to the Divine ideal of perfection.

CHAPTER V

RELIGIOUS CONSCIOUSNESS

Diagram (2) Percept II.—Natural phenomena suggest spiritual noumena—Nature the first teacher of religion—Causality, utility, and directivity—Beauty, unlimited expanse, and the infinite—The grand and terrible—The Idea of God—Dreams and the ghost theory.

NATURAL PHENOMENA SUGGEST SPIRITUAL NOUMENA

THE objects and activities of the outer natural world perceived by the bodily senses are by the nerves conveyed to the brain, where by the faculty of apperception they give rise to (1) mental ideas and concepts, (2) to spiritual noumena, and (3) to religious consciousness.

Here the transition from percept to concept is comparatively simple and easy to understand. The number of objects embraced under the head of natural phenomena is unlimited, and I have only endeavoured to give two or three examples with the corresponding concepts to which they have given rise.

NATURE THE FIRST TEACHER OF RELIGION

There appears little doubt that in all ages, and amongst all races of mankind, Nature herself has been the first great teacher of religion; that through Nature, and the phenomena and activities of Nature, perceived by the senses, the religious instinct and consciousness have been first awakened.

The beauty and loveliness of Nature, varied at times by sights and sounds of impressive grandeur and sublimity; the terrific forces of Nature displayed in flood or tempest or lightning shaft; the forces of Nature heard in the thunder-crash which seems to shake the heavens, or the rumbling of the earthquake striking terror into the hearts of men; these and such-like phenomena could never fail to impress the human imagination, not only with fear, but with a sense of the supernatural, and suggest the idea of a power and personality behind and beyond Nature which, though unseen, was not the less real.

It is easy, I think, to understand how such percepts as these would, through apperception, beget the concept of a Divine Being or beings to be feared, propitiated, and worshipped. The people of Fiji regard shooting stars as gods, and the smaller ones as the departing souls of men.[4]

And here, before going further, I should like to turn aside for a moment to call attention to that remarkable utterance of St. Paul in Rom. i. 20. The passage in the R.V. reads thus—

"For the invisible things of Him since the creation of the world are clearly seen, being

[4] Max Müller's "Hibbert Lectures," p. 86.

perceived through the things that are made, even His everlasting power and divinity." [1]

St. Paul was not only a Christian, but a philosopher, and in this passage, which we may almost regard as classic for its intimate bearing on the subject before us, if he does not definitely formulate the thesis of the Spiritual Philosophy, he not obscurely indicates one of its fundamental canons.

In "*the things that are made*" we have the percepts of natural phenomena and activity; in "*the invisible things*" we have the mental concepts, the Divine ideas, or *noumena*; and in "*the everlasting power and divinity*" we have the consummation of all ideas and spiritual noumena in the one great central all-embracing *Idea of God*.

It was thus, according to St. Paul, that religious consciousness came to its birth. To express it in terms of modern psychology, we should say that primary concepts arising from the perception of natural phenomena lead on to secondary noumena, and these, when gathered up and focussed on the screen of human psychic intelligence, beget the Idea of God and religious consciousness.

BIRTH OF RELIGIOUS CONSCIOUSNESS

"We may safely say," says Prof. Max Müller,[2] "that, in spite of all researches, no human beings

---

[1] The Greek brings out the meaning more clearly : Τὰ γὰρ ἀόρατα αὐτοῦ ἀπὸ κτίσεως κόσμου τοῖς ποιήμασι νοούμενα καθορᾶται ἥ τε ἀΐδιος αὐτοῦ δύναμις καὶ θειότης.

[2] Hibbert Lectures on "The Origin and Growth of Religion," p. 79.

have been found anywhere who do not possess something which to them is religion; or, to put it in the most general form, a belief in something beyond what they can see with their eyes. It is legitimate, therefore, to call religion, in its most general sense an universal phenomenon of humanity."

To the ancient seers and poets of India the dawn of day seemed like a divinity opening the golden gates of another world. And while these gates were open for the sun to pass in triumph, their eyes and their mind strove in their childish way to pierce beyond the limits of this finite world.

The Vedic poets gave it the name of Aditi, the Boundless, the Yonder, the Beyond all and everything.[1]

The percepts which come under the head of natural phenomena are, as I have said, far too numerous to mention. In the diagram, therefore, I have selected only a few of the more important.

After the remarks I have already made on this step in the process of psychic evolution, a few explanatory notes would seem to be all that are necessary to make this portion of the diagram intelligible.

Let us take the percepts in the order in which they are placed.

[1] "Hymn to Mitra and Varuna," thus translated by Max Müller: "You mount your chariot, which at the dawning of the Dawn is golden-coloured and has iron poles at the setting of the sun (gold and iron)."

(*a*) The regular sequence of cause and effect begets the primary concept of *causality* as the primary concept; of the necessary existence of a Prime Cause, a *Causa Causarum*, as the secondary concept.

(*b*) UTILITY, DIRECTIVITY, AND DESIGN

The observation of utility and directivity in Nature begets the idea of purpose and design, which in turn leads on to the concept and inference of an intelligent Mind or Author; an Artificer, Who is working behind the processes of Nature with a definite and beneficent object in view.

(*c*) BEAUTY

Concrete forms of beauty, and especially the marvellous beauty displayed in the physical structures of plants and flowers and animals, give rise to the mental concept of abstract beauty as distinct from utility; and this, again, as a secondary concept, to the idea of a Being Who is the complexion of all that is beautiful.

The following passage occurs in Plato's "Symposium." It is so germane to the subject under discussion, and so aptly illustrates my meaning, that I make no apology for reproducing it:—

". . . And the true order of going, or being led by another, to the things of love, is to begin from the beauties of earth and mount upwards for the sake of that other beauty, using these as steps only, and from one going on to two, and from two to all fair forms, and from fair forms to fair practices, and from fair practices to fair notions, until from fair notions he arrives at the notion of absolute beauty, and at last knows what the essence of beauty is. . . . But what if man had eyes to see the true beauty—the divine beauty, I mean, pure and clear and unalloyed, not clogged with the pollution of mortality, and all the colours and vanities of human life—thither looking, and holding converse with the true beauty simple and divine? Remember how, in that communion only, beholding beauty with the eye of the mind, he will be enabled to bring forth, not *images* of beauty but *realities* (for he has hold, not of an image, but of a reality), and bringing forth and nourishing true virtue to become the friend of God and be immortal, if mortal may. Would that be an ignoble life?"

With such a passage as this before him, well might the late Prof. W. James say, "Abstract beauty is for Plato a perfectly definite individual being, of which the intellect is aware, as of something additional to all the 'perishing beauties of the earth.'"[1]

(d) Unlimited Expanse—the Infinite

The percept of unlimited expanse, as in the boundless ocean, or the unfathomable depths of

[1] "Varieties of Religious Experience," p. 57.

stellar space, may well have begotten the idea of infinity. And to these may now be added that wonderful all-pervading substance, if that be the right word to use, which Sir O. Lodge has done much to elucidate. No one surely can read his book, "The Ether of Space," without feeling that his previous idea of the infinite universe has been expanded and enriched. The Universe is no longer an empty void, peopled with isolated and independent bodies, but a unit, bound together by a mysterious tie which brings them all into touch as members of the same great family.

(*e*) THE GRAND AND TERRIBLE

The grand, the terrible, the abnormal, give rise to the concept of the Supernatural as the primary, and this again to the Sublime as the secondary concept.

The list of percepts of natural phenomena and activities, and their corresponding ideas or concepts might be still further extended, but those I have specified will suffice for my purpose.

There needs but one further step in the apperceptive process, namely, the synthesis of these ideas, and the attribution of them to one great central, all-embracing Cause, and we arrive at the idea of God and the origin of the religious consciousness in man.

Of course, it is almost needless to point out that the forms of natural religion in which the religious consciousness has manifested itself in various countries, and amongst different races of men, have been many and various—from mere fetishism and idolatry, through polytheism, pantheism, and mythology, up to the higher forms, such as Buddhism, Brahminism, and even Monotheism. All these, terrible and revolting as some of them are, bear witness to the universal prevalence of the religious instinct and consciousness.

The acquisition of this faculty was a step forward in the psychic development in man, by which he became capable of receiving those fuller, clearer intimations of the Divine Nature which were yet to come.

Dreams and Ghost Theory

I would not for a moment deny that other agencies and percepts besides those generated by natural phenomena may also have exercised considerable influence in the formation of the religious concept and consciousness. For example, Charles Darwin was disposed to think, that through dreams the religious concept was first quickened. Others, again, have attributed its origin to a belief in ghosts and the spirits of departed friends and ancestors. There may be some truth in both suppositions. Still, I think their influence must have been small compared with that arising from the perception of the ordinary and extraordinary phenomena of Nature.

"THE theory of evolution has thrown not a little light on the problem of the existence of moral evil in the world. We are able to understand now, in a way that was not possible before the theory of development was reached, that moral evil is rather failure on man's part to rise higher in the scale of being and to respond to the true dignity of his nature, than a fall from a state of perfection which was his when he started upon his history. The interpretation of the Fall of Man has been greatly modified by the scientific conclusions of modern times. But there is perhaps a danger in our day lest an apparently simple explanation of the fact of moral evil should lessen man's sense of responsibility, and the claims of conscience should be neglected or explained away."—Dr. E. H. Askwith, "Sin and the Need of Atonement" (*Cambridge Theological Essays*), p. 177.

CHAPTER VI

MORAL CONSCIOUSNESS

Diagram No. 2, Percept III.—Ethical distinctions—The problem of good and evil—Views of Kant, Wundt, and W. James—Antithesis and its relation to psychical development—A note of congruity.

THE next step in psychic development is that by which moral consciousness is added to the previous acquisitions of self-consciousness and religious consciousness. This, again, as before, is due to the faculty of apperception applied to another class of percepts—the observation of distinctions and antitheses; not this time of the physical and material, but of the ethical and spiritual order, and the result is the primary concept of moral law.

ETHICAL DISTINCTIONS

That these distinctions are real, and stand for antagonistic moral and spiritual principles or forces which underlie them, most people, I imagine, are prepared to admit. And yet there are those who would invoke the "absence" theory to explain away the antithesis and active hostility between good and evil. Evil, they say, is a nonentity, and only the negation or absence of good. Sin is vanity, and vanity is emptiness. So neither evil nor sin has any real existence.

Might we not as well say, "There is no such thing as bitterness, for bitterness is only the absence of sweetness"? But in water there is an absence of sweetness, and yet it is not bitter. The South Pole is the negative of the North Pole. Shall we say, then, that the South Pole has no existence? What would our astronomers say to such an assertion? By such reasoning it is possible to deny the existence of sin and pain, and even death itself. But such a denial, beside being contrary to common sense and experience, is unphilosophical, and argues the inability to see that the "positive" requires the negative as its complement, and that both are realities necessary to complete the "whole." And we know "evil" not only as the negation, or absence, of "good," but as its antithesis and opponent.

The Problem of Good and Evil

Into the cause of these ethical distinctions and antagonisms I do not propose to enter. We can neither deny nor explain them. They constitute a mystery, which it is beyond the power of human intelligence or intuition to solve. Even Kant himself was of this opinion, and insisted that the trouble expended in seeking a solution was "only so much time and labour wasted."[1]

[1] "The question of evil is as old as humanity itself. It enters into all forms of religion. It is the background of all mystery in human life, and its shadow falls even on that outer world of cosmical law, which seems most removed from it."—"The Christian Doctrine of Sin," by Principal Tulloch, p. 29.

Professor Wundt

Like Kant, Prof. Wundt declines to discuss the problem of the existence side by side of moral good and evil; but he recognizes the reality of the strife, and argues that it is due to the antagonism between "wills" which can only be terminated by the harmonizing of all will-forms with the supreme will of God.[1]

It is almost superfluous to point out that this view of the conflict between good and evil is one which, with some slight alterations and reservations, could easily be accepted as that of the Spiritual Philosophy.

To me, I confess, it seems the merest trifling to deny or ignore the distinction and antagonism between good and evil, however unable we may be to explain it. To deny the existence of evil as an active principle in the world is to run counter to the fundamental law of vital evolution, namely, struggle between opposing forces, and survival of the fittest.[2]

---

[1] "The conflict of good and evil is just this strife between wills. Since the empirical social will is finite and liable to error, the ultimate solution of this conflict is to be found only in an idea of reason, which makes the infinite series of will-forms terminate in a Supreme will, phenomenally manifest in the individual consciousness as the imperative of the moral ideal in the State, and in society as the spirit of history, and in the religious conception of the world as the Divine will."—"Principles of Morality," p. 112.

[2] For a synopsis of the various theories of the problem of good and evil, and further remarks on it, see Appendix A.

Pragmatist View

Of the obligations we owe to the late Prof. W. James, not the least is this, that he has taught us the value of Pragmatism as a solvent for problems in philosophy and metaphysic which would otherwise appear insoluble. Obstacles which defy a frontal attack may, sometimes, be circumvented and overcome by a flank movement.

The problem of evil is one of those obstacles, and I think it may interest my readers to hear how Prof. James regarded it.

"The method of averting one's attention from evil, *i.e.* of ignoring it, and living simply in the light of good,[1] is splendid as long as it will work. . . . But it breaks down impotently as soon as melancholy comes, and even though one be quite free from melancholy oneself, there is no doubt that healthy-mindedness is inadequate as a philosophic doctrine, because the evil facts which it refuses positively to account for are *a genuine portion of reality*; and they may be, after all, the best key to life's significance, and possibly be the only openers of our eyes to the deepest levels of truth."[2]

I think this is profoundly true. He goes on as follows:—

"The normal process of life contains moments as bad as any of those which insane melancholy is filled with, moments in which radical evil gets its

---
[1] James is referring to the optimism of Emerson.
[2] "Varieties of Religious Experience."

innings and takes its solid turn. . . . Here on our very hearths and in our gardens, the infernal cat plays with the panting mouse, or holds the hot bird fluttering in her jaws. It may be that no religious reconciliation with the absolute totality of things is possible. Some evils, indeed, are ministerial to higher forms of good; but it may be that there are forms of evil so extreme as to enter into no good system whatever, and that, in respect of such evil, dumb submission, or neglect to notice, is the only practical resource."[1]

So far Prof. James. And I fully agree with him. I cannot think that any real advance in our knowledge of the problem of evil will ever be gained by shutting our eyes to the facts of daily experience, or attempting to deny or explain away the inference to which they point, namely, that evil is as much a reality as good.

For this reason, it seems to me that the better plan of dealing with this great problem will be to regard it from the evolutional point of view. No one, I think, will deny that under that system of evolution we live and move and have our being. We ourselves, as we exist to-day, intelligent, moral, psychical beings, are the product, and so far the highest product, of that system. Is it not, therefore, more in accordance with true philosophy, and even common sense, that we should first study, and, if possible, ascertain the laws of vital

[1] "Varieties of Religious Experience," pp. 164, 165.

development, which by their action have made us what we are, rather than entangle and perplex ourselves with metaphysical subtleties and theological speculations, which, after all, may only land us in contradictions we cannot reconcile, because they involve a mystery which lies beyond the reach of our finite intelligence?

ANTITHESIS

We observe, then, in the first place, that antithesis forms the substratum, so to speak, on which the whole process of evolution rests. Life in all its phases and stages of development, whether physical or psychical, is a struggle, a life-and-death struggle, between the powers of good and evil. And the organism, be it the lowly amœba or the self-conscious soul of man, that will not face the struggle, or is worsted in it, is bound to go under. It would be possible to imagine a perfect world—a world, that is, in which there was no evil, and nothing but good. We shall do well to remember, however, that such a world would not be one of our order, not an evolutional world, a world in the making, but a world already made and perfected. But our world is evolutional, a world still in the making and imperfect, but advancing towards a possible perfection so far as regards the human race, through the struggle between good and evil.[1]

[1] "I for one feel rationally assured that a free action of the human intelligence and will, under the influences to which humanity is

Nature herself is not an ever-smiling, beneficent dame. She can be very angry, very cruel. Sometimes she slays her own offspring, and brings others to the birth, a foul brood, instinct only with devilish hatred and hostility to every form of life except their own. Sometimes she turns her hand upon herself, as when the frosts in spring cut off the blossoms and destroy the promise of the year; as when the volcano belches forth its tongues of lurid flame and devastates the fertile plain with streams of liquid lava;[1] when the deluge of waters sweeps the harvest from the fields, or the summer drought brings famine and death to millions of innocent creatures. Even vital energy itself has fallen under the spell of antithesis, and we see malefic forms of life as prolific and active as the good and beneficent. The deadly serpent and the harmless dove are alike the product of evolution, and humanity finds its work cut out in fighting against the insidious microbes of disease and death. How strange all this must sound in the ears of the optimist or Christian scientist, who would fain persuade himself and us that all is for the best in this best of possible worlds; that there is no such thing as

subjected (in its environment) is among the agencies that serve the purposes of God, and for which in His plans allowance is made."— *Hibbert Journal*, July, 1913, art. "Evil."

[1] After the recent earthquake at Messina, a man was observed raising his clenched hand to heaven, and exclaiming, "O God, if Thou dost exist, why dost Thou permit such an awful catastrophe as this to happen?"

evil, or that, at the worst, it is only the negation or absence of the good.

Nor may we suppose that this antithesis, this antagonism between good and evil, is only to be found in the lower forms of animal life. It persists throughout the whole range of vital and psychical evolution, whether moral, religious, or spiritual. Each new manifestation [1] of the Spirit by which the content of the self-conscious Ego is increased is given under the form of antithesis expressed and guarded by its corresponding law. In each succeeding stage the contrast between good and evil becomes deepened and intensified. But in every one the condition of life, as a struggle between the opposing forces of good and evil, remains the same; and in every one, psychical and spiritual progress, or the reverse, depends on the issue of the conflict. If, when a higher moral or spiritual ideal is conceived, men refuse to respond to it, and choose rather the lower life of mere animal propensity and lust, or if, while consenting to a moral law, they refuse a higher spiritual law, should such be subsequently revealed, then in both cases sin comes in and tends to defeat the purpose of God.

[1] "The ideal of the whole (moral development) is not something completed, something given once for all; it is always in process of becoming, and never finished. The moral consciousness of every age comprehends it in certain ends, motives, and laws. The true value of these last, however, consists not in their absolute but in their relative permanence; in the fact that they really share in the general process of development whose coherence is demonstrated by the steadily increasing perfection of moral ideas. It is not until this final stage, when ideal motives rule, that we get clearly conscious morality."—"The Principles of Morality," p. 70, Prof. Wundt.

A Note of Congruity

But, though we cannot solve the mystery of evil, we should not lose sight of the fact, that an environment consisting of both good and evil is that which is best fitted to secure the further progress, psychical and spiritual, of such a creature as man, possessed both of the faculty to perceive ethical distinctions, and freedom to choose between them.

Destroy the power of choice and free will, and man ceases to be a moral agent. Destroy the presence and antagonism of good and evil in his surroundings, and you remove the very condition on which psychical development depends.

But such a moral Being as we conceive God to be cannot be served by compulsion, but only with the willing assent of intelligence and love.

And lastly, we perceive that the law of psychical and spiritual evolution, which we see actually in operation, contains within it the possibilities of indefinite progress and expansion. For as the concept of moral worth springs ultimately from the manifestation of God, whether in nature or revelation, so the advance towards moral perfection has nothing to limit it but such fuller manifestation of Himself as the Deity may be pleased to make, on the one hand, and the response of mankind thereto, on the other.

In the next chapter the primary and secondary concepts arising from the percept of ethical distinctions will come under consideration.

"THE process by which a man becomes conscious of his own personality is essentially a metaphysical process, and without the conscious recognition of personality there can be no sense of duty, no individual ethics. The same process leads to the recognition of other personalities, and is the basis of social ethics—the individual's duty to others—the duty of members of a society to one another."—" Ethical Significance of Christian Doctrines," J. F. Bethune-Baker, D.D., *Cambridge Theological Essays*, p. 535.

CHAPTER VII

MORAL CONSCIOUSNESS—*continued*

Primary concept: Moral Law—Secondary concepts: Duty, Responsibility, Sin, and Penalty.

EVOLUTION OF MORAL CONSCIOUSNESS

THE subject of the origin and development of moral consciousness is by no means a simple and easy one. It is one on which much has been written and a great diversity of opinion exists amongst students of human psychology.

Prof. Wundt, of Leipzig University, has discussed it in his Ethics at great length and with great ability. And before him Immanuel Kant, in his "Critique of Pure Reason," treated it with his usual acumen. My object is not to criticize their conclusions, but only to examine the subject under the light of the Spiritual Philosophy.

For every form of life, and at every stage of vital development, from the amœba right up to man, there exists an objective environment in which the good and the bad, the beneficial and the injurious, are intermingled. The organism must choose between the two, and according to its choice will ascend or descend in the scale of life and well-being. But as in the process of evolution organisms become more highly developed, the faculty of choice tends to become less and less instinctive and automatic, and more and more intelligent, ethical, and free. At the same time, and under the same process of evolution, the objects, good and bad, between which a choice has to be made tend to acquire a more ethical character.

But, if it be true that concept, or idea, is the production in the region of consciousness of the *reality* of which the objective percept was only the symbol, then it follows that, as the distinction and antithesis between the good and the bad assumes a more ethical character, the concept of the good, that is, the moral consciousness, will undergo a corresponding increase in tone and value.

To this process of enrichment it is clear there can be but one limit, and that limit will only be reached when the fullest manifestation of goodness and truth has been made to man by the immanent Spirit of God, and the human moral consciousness has become assimilated to the Divine Idea of the Good.

And here it is where Prof. Wundt and his immortal predecessor Kant part company. For while the latter regarded the moral consciousness as implying a will which can will what it ought— as the expression of "an original and unconditioned imperative to act *so* and not *otherwise*," the former holds that the Kantian view of duty as God-given once for all and inherent in the human mind, is "a reconstruction of the old mythological theory of conscience, and otherwise objectionable because it conflicts both with moral experience and the psychological nature of man."[1]

This discrepancy of opinion is not to be wondered at, when we remember that in Kant's day psychology, as a branch of science, was little known and studied. Moral problems were regarded mainly, if not solely, from an intellectual and metaphysical point of view, while the modern theory of evolution had scarcely been heard of. It is very different now. The truth and universality of evolution have become generally recognized, and are believed to hold good, not only in the domain of physics and biology, but also in those of psychology, morality, and religion.

What the effect this new method of investigating moral problems has been in modifying previous views and theories of moral consciousness will be best expressed in Prof. Wundt's own words—

"For the ideal of the whole (moral consciousness) is not something completed, something given once for all; it is always in process of becoming, and never finished. The consciousness of every age comprehends it in certain ends, motives, and laws. The true value of these last, however,

[1] Wundt, "The Principles of Morality," p. 62, Eng. translation.

consists not in their absolute, but in their relative permanence; in the fact that they really share in the general process of development whose coherence is demonstrated by the steadily increasing perfection of moral ideas. It is not until this final stage is reached, when ideal motives rule, that we get clearly conscious morality." [1]

I scarcely need point out that this view of the German professor abundantly confirms my contention in this section, that the moral consciousness is a thing of slow growth, but of indefinite expansion.[2]

The fact is that moral percept and concept are closely related, and in a sense act and react on each other. Each higher moral percept calls forth a corresponding higher concept to increase the content and raise the character of the moral consciousness. And each increase and appreciation of the moral consciousness prepares and fits it for a higher manifestation of goodness and truth, *i.e.* a further revelation of the Spirit of Divine wisdom immanent in the Universe.

[1] " Principles of Morality," p. 70.

[2] " In the earliest conceptions of law we find the merest germs of our present ideas on the subject, and in its further evolution, law, like every other intellectual creation, is affected by national tendencies and historical events. Even social, political, and philosophical theories have not been without their influence on this development. . . ."— Wundt's " Principles of Morality," p. 160.

Primary Concept—Moral Law

I have been endeavouring to show that the concept or idea of Moral Law, which forms the basis of moral consciousness, rests on the essential ethical difference and antagonism between the good and the bad, the true and the false, and the innate power of the self-conscious soul to perceive this difference and antagonism.

But it would be a mistake to suppose that moral law is the only kind of law which by the process of evolution has been disclosed. It would be far truer to say that law has been the invariable concomitant of every stage of the evolutionary process. This is almost a self-evident proposition, which needs only to be stated and not proved. Physical phenomena, such as the force of gravity, electrical energy, chemical affinity, etc., are all subject to laws which we call the laws of physics.

Next in order would come the laws which govern the development of animal and vegetable life.

In the lower stages of life, where the organism performs its functions automatically and instinctively, we find that instinct itself acts in obedience to fixed laws which we call the laws of Nature, chief among which is the law of self-preservation. As the organism develops, it tends to act less and less from instinct, and more and more from intelligence. But it does not thereby escape from the restraints of law. Here a higher law awaits it, the Moral Law, which springs from the percept of ethical distinctions. Of this there is no need to speak, as we have already had it under consideration.

When primitive man lived a solitary life and roamed the forest in pursuit of game, he seemed free from law; he was his own master and a law unto himself. But as soon as he began to live the tribal or community life, he quickly found his freedom curtailed. Such a life was only possible under the restrictions of social law. Such laws would be founded on a perception of the difference between *meum* and *tuum*, between honesty and fraud, and would safeguard life and property against crime and violence, cruelty and injustice, and inflict punishment on the offenders.

The recent discovery of the Code of Hammurabi,[1] which dates back to some time about 2200

---

[1] Hammurabi was probably the Amraphel of Gen. xiv. 1. He was the sixth king of the first known dynasty of Babylon, and reigned for forty-three years about 2150 B.C. While excavating at Susa in 1901, M. de Morgan discovered a large stone with a bas-relief representing Hammurabi receiving a code of laws from Shamash the Sun-god. The laws relate to a great variety of subjects, such, for example, as the possession and inheritance of property, the duties and privileges of royal servants and others, the rights of wife and children, the rates of wages, etc. Of this Code Dr. Driver says, " The provisions are never of a ritual or ceremonial character, they relate to what we call civil and criminal law, and a considerable number of them are remarkably similar to corresponding provisions of the Hebrew codes preserved in the Pentateuch."—"Modern Research as illustrating the Bible," pp. 26, 27.

B.C., and is, I believe, the oldest moral code in existence, gives countenance to this view.

But while it seems probable that in the social and communal life, the idea of Moral Law first took its rise and began by apperception to assume a rudimentary form of moral consciousness, it did not end there. It was destined to take on a nobler character, and receive a higher sanction when in the course of evolutionary progress worthier ideals of truth and goodness, with their corresponding antitheses, should be revealed.

As the percept of ethical distinctions becomes more clear and comprehensive, so in exact proportion does the concept of Moral Law increase in range and obligation; until at last it is seen to embrace and rule all the relationships of life, not only the relationship of man to his fellows, but the relationship of man to God, who is the Author and End of his being.

Secondary or Inferential Concepts

The secondary concepts to which the primary concept of Moral Law gives rise are: Duty, Responsibility, Sin, and Penalty. Let me take them in this order.

Duty

That the recognition of a Moral Law which carries its own authority and obligation along with it, begets the sense of Duty, is an obvious truth.

For what is duty? It is something which "I ought to do." And, if there be a law which stands for the distinction between good and evil, which approves the former and condemns the latter, then both natural instinct and self-interest tell me, with a categorical imperative,[1] that I ought to obey that law.

Responsibility

Closely akin to the sense of duty, and springing immediately from it, is that of responsibility. For if, while conscious of a law which I recognize it my duty to obey, I voluntarily and intentionally refuse to do so, I make myself responsible for all the consequences which may ensue from such disobedience. And this responsibility is threefold. If the law is intended to safeguard the duty I owe to myself, then to myself I am responsible. If it relates to the duty I owe to society, to society I am responsible for the breach of duty in this respect. And, lastly, if there be a Lawgiver behind the law, as doubtless there is, who is able to vindicate His law, to Him also I am responsible.

Sin

As Duty stands for obedience to the moral law, and indeed to law in general, so Sin stands for the

---

[1] Prof. Wundt recognizes four imperative motives or constraints: (1) External constraint; (2) internal; (3) permanent satisfaction; (4) the conception of an ideal moral life. The last of these corresponds to the concept of moral law.

infraction of law, and is therefore the antithesis of duty.

There are many synonyms for sin in the Indo-European languages, for the discussion of which I must refer my readers to Appendix Note C. Few of them, however, etymologically considered, are possessed of true ethical significance. And it is the concept of moral law which finally imparts to them this significance of moral defect.

From the concept of sin as the infraction of law, the following inferences and conclusions necessarily follow :—

(1) Where there is no law there can be no sin. For sin is the transgression of the law.

(2) According to the character of the law, such is the character of the sin of disobeying it.

(3) So long as there is wilful disobedience to law, so long is there sin.

(4) Only by obedience to law of whatever kind can sin be eliminated.

(5) Animals below the rank of man cannot sin, because they are conscious only of natural law, which their instinct prompts them to obey. But man can sin, because he both can recognize higher forms of law and has free will to choose whether he will obey or disobey them.[1]

[1] Since writing the above I have come across the following passage in the Rev. C. Moxon's article on "The Christian Idea of God and Recent Thought," which appears in the *Contemporary Review* for May, 1913. It is so pertinent to the subject under discussion, that I need make no apology for quoting it.

"Sin," he says, "is due to the dawning consciousness of a higher

According to the teaching of the Spiritual Philosophy, each stage in the process of vital and psychic evolution is due ultimately to the Spirit of Divine wisdom, revealing with ever-growing clearness the radical distinction and antithesis between good and evil, and guiding the creature aright by the institution of congruous laws.

The law says, "This is the way, walk ye in it, for it will lead you to life and happiness. But sin is disobedience and rebellion against law, and can only lead you to misery and death."

Penalty

This secondary concept follows as a necessary and logical corollary to the three we have already noticed, namely, duty, responsibility, and sin. Unless the concept of law be a mere imaginary fiction, it must entail the idea of reward and punishment. It must be so. For the law which was not armed with judicial and executive power would cease to be a law at all, for no one would respect it. In some cases the connection between law and punishment is so immediate and obvious that none can fail to see it. Those who will dare to violate the laws of Nature soon find that she can avenge herself with speedy and inexorable severity. So, too, with the laws of social

set of laws, and the consequent clash with lower laws of human and animal nature. Sin occurs when the selfish desires are not ruled by the higher demands of consciousness."

and civil life. And if in the case of other and higher forms of law the connection is less obvious and direct, when virtue seems to go unrewarded and vice unpunished, we may not doubt that judgment and punishment, though they be delayed, will eventually take place, if not in this sublunary sphere of existence, then in one which is yet to come. In law we must recognize the voice of the Lawgiver, Who will not fail to vindicate Himself in His own due time and way.

"In order to reveal to men the Divine life under the conditions of human life, the Son of God Himself became man—accepting whatever limitations were necessary, in order that His life on earth as man should be a really human life. The life He lived on earth was one of service, entailing suffering—even a painful form of death. The whole purpose of it was ethical—to reveal to men the ideal life, and so to stir in them the will to live that life, and give them power to carry out that will."—" Ethical Significance of Christian Doctrines," by Rev. J. F. Bethune-Baker, D.D., *Cambridge Theological Essays*, p. 552.

CHAPTER VIII

THE INCARNATION AND SPIRITUAL CONSCIOUSNESS

Percept IV.—The Incarnation considered under a threefold aspect: (*a*) The *a priori* point of view—(*b*) As presented in the Gospel records—(*c*) As indicated by the claims which Jesus made for Himself.

HITHERTO my aim has been to trace the successive steps whereby the animal psychè has been transformed into the personal self-conscious soul, or Ego, of man as we now know him to be.

(1) Starting from consciousness as the common characteristic of vital organisms, I endeavoured to show how the percept of consciousness in other forms of life led by apperception to the concept of self-consciousness.

(2) How the percept of natural phenomena by the same process gave birth to spiritual noumena and religious consciousness.

(3) How the percept of ethical distinction and antagonisms begat the concept of moral law and moral consciousness, finding its expression in the faculty and function of conscience.

We now come to the consideration of the further step in psychical development, resulting from the percept of the Incarnation regarded as a direct manifestation of the creative Logos in the Person of Jesus Christ.[1]

The Incarnation

The whole subject is one of such vast and vital importance in connection with the system of Spiritual Philosophy, that no apology is needed for treating it with some detail. I propose, therefore, to consider the Incarnation under the following heads :—

(*a*) The Incarnation regarded from an *a priori* point of view.

(*b*) As presented to us in the Gospel records ; *i.e.* the claims made in behalf of Jesus by His followers.

(*c*) As indicated by the claims which Jesus made for Himself.

(*a*) The *a priori* View

Assuming for the moment the truth of our contention that the phenomena of Nature and the gradual evolution of life are due to the Divine

---

[1] Here let me call attention to column I. on the extreme left of Diagram No. 2. All percepts are due to the Divine energy immanent and active in the Universe through the creative Logos and the Hokmah, or Holy Spirit. But these percepts are of two kinds: those marked A, which arise in the ordinary course of natural and psychic evolution without the direct intervention of any supernatural cause; secondly, those marked B, which are of a metaphysical nature ; and thirdly, those marked C, which are of an abnormal character, and cannot be accounted for except through the agency of a supernatural cause. To this latter class percepts IV. and V. belong.

Energy immanent in the Universe through the creative Logos; and secondly, that the final purpose or highest value of that evolutionary process is to be found in the psychical development of mankind, which thus becomes assimilated to the Divine nature; assuming all this, is there anything unreasonable or improbable in the supposition that the same Divine Energy should, in continuation of the evolutionary process, and for the attainment of the same object, manifest Himself in a yet clearer, more direct, and personal manner, even by assuming human nature itself?

On the contrary, is it not probable on *a priori* grounds that such a manifestation should be made? Look at what has been already accomplished under the evolutionary process. We have seen the conscious animal psychè transformed into the self-conscious Ego of man. To this has been added the religious consciousness, and to this again the faculty of moral consciousness, until we have in man a creature capable of knowing God, and yearning to know Him; of perceiving the ethical distinction between good and evil, of approving the former and condemning the latter.

That all this has been accomplished under the process of evolution cannot be denied. Was it not, then, to be expected that a further and fuller revelation of the Divine nature should be made to carry forward the work of psychical development to a higher level, unless we are to suppose that in man, as we know him, evolution has reached its highest point and come to an end ?

But such a supposition seems in the highest degree improbable. Man cannot rest where he is, on a sort of spiritual inclined plane. He must ascend, or he must descend. If he is to ascend, then it can only be by the provision of such a new environment as will afford both stimulus and satisfaction to his psychical faculties and capacities. But is not this just what the Incarnation claims to do ?

I submit, then, that there is no objection to be urged against the Incarnation on the *a priori* grounds of reason and probability. God has ever been speaking to man though the operations of Nature and the voice of conscience. The only difference is that through the Incarnation He has spoken with a clearer voice and a more direct and personal manner, as soon as man was able to hear and understand it.

(*b*) THE CLAIMS MADE ON BEHALF OF JESUS BY HIS DISCIPLES

It must be admitted at the outset that these claims are of a supernatural order.

In the first place, it is claimed for the Incarnation that it was a manifestation, in human nature, of the Logos or Word of God; that in the Person of Jesus Christ two whole and perfect natures, the human and Divine, were united, without blending or confusion, each one retaining its integrity and perfection. All this is set forth in the plainest and briefest terms in the first chapter of the Fourth Gospel—

"In the beginning was the Word, and the Word was with God, and the Word was God... All things were made by Him; and without Him was not anything made that hath been made.... He was in the world [immanent in the universe],... and the world knew Him not. He came unto His own, and His own received Him not... And the Word became (ἐγένετο) flesh, and tabernacled among us (and we beheld His glory, glory as of the Only-begotten from the Father), full of grace and truth" (John i. 1–14, R.V.).

Moreover, it is claimed for Jesus that His Incarnation not only was foretold by the Jewish prophets, speaking under the inspiration of the Holy Ghost; but also that in its inception, provection, and completion the same Holy Spirit played a most important part. Thus, in the Gospel of St. Luke, we read: "The Holy Ghost shall come upon thee, and the power of the Highest shall overshadow thee, therefore also that Holy Thing which shall be born of thee shall be called the Son of God" (Luke i. 35).

Again, in the Gospel of St. Matthew: "Joseph, thou son of David, fear not to take unto thee Mary thy wife: for that which is conceived in her is of the Holy Ghost. And she shall bring forth a son, and thou shalt call His name Jesus [Saviour]: for He shall save His people from their sins" (Matt. i. 20, 21).

At His Baptism we are told that "the heavens were opened unto Him, and He saw the Spirit of God descending like a dove, and lighting upon Him. And lo a voice from heaven saying, This is My beloved Son, in Whom I am well pleased" (Matt. iii. 16, 17; cf. Isa. i. 2 and xlii. 1).

Moreover, it is claimed for Jesus not only that He was wonderfully born, but that He was invested with a superhuman power to work miracles, and that He exercised this power in various ways and on many occasions during the three years of His ministry. He fed the multitudes in the wilderness, healed the sick, gave sight to the blind, and even raised the dead to life again.

At last, having been condemned to death through the malice of His enemies, He expired on the cross; but after three days He rose again, and appeared on many occasions to His disciples and Apostles, who never expected to see Him alive again.

Finally, after remaining on earth forty days, during which He was giving instruction and commandments to His chosen followers the Apostles, He was parted from them and in their presence ascended into heaven.

Such are some of the principal claims that are

made on behalf of Jesus by the writers of the Gospel records. It is needless to point out that they are altogether of a superhuman and miraculous nature. They are contrary to our ordinary experience, and the conclusion of Nicodemus was not only just, but afforded the only alternative to utter scepticism : " No man can do the miracles Thou doest, except God be with Him." There are two alternatives open to mankind—either to admit the claims put forth in the Gospel records on behalf of Jesus, or to reject them. If they are admitted, then Nicodemus was right : " God was with Him." If they are rejected, this means such a mutilation of the Gospel story as would leave it both incoherent and unintelligible. That story, as it seems to me, must be accepted or rejected as a whole. For to attempt to eliminate the miraculous element, and yet retain the rest, would be like trying to remove the pattern from a carpet, or a piece of tapestry, by drawing out the threads which compose it, and still expect the fabric to retain its use and beauty.

(c) THE CLAIMS WHICH JESUS MADE FOR HIMSELF

In considering these claims it will be convenient to arrange them under two heads.

A. What Jesus claimed to be, *i.e.* His Personality and Character.

B. What Jesus claimed to do, *i.e.* His mission and His work.

A. What Jesus claimed to be

(1) *The Claim to fulfil Prophecy*

It will hardly be disputed that in the Old Testament Scriptures we do find a long series of predictions all pointing forward to the advent of One Who, as the Anointed (Messiah) of God, should fulfil them. Up to the time of Jesus no one had claimed to do this. But when He came, He boldly and habitually claimed to fulfil all the Old Testament prophecies which were held to be Messianic. On one occasion we read of His going into the little synagogue at Nazareth, where He had been brought up, on the sabbath day, and turning to the Book of Isaiah, and reading one of the most striking of the evangelical predictions—

"The Spirit of the Lord is upon Me, because He anointed Me to preach good tidings to the poor: He hath sent Me to proclaim release to the captives, and recovering of sight to the blind, to set at liberty them that are bruised, to proclaim the acceptable year of the Lord" (Isa. lxi. 1, 2).

And then, with these words for His text, He began to tell them, "To-day hath this scripture been fulfilled in your ears."[1]

(2) *A Teacher come from God*

Jesus claimed to be a Teacher, but such a Teacher as the world had never seen before, and

[1] Luke iv. 21. See also Matt. viii. 17; xii. 6, 15.

THE CLAIMS OF JESUS

has never seen since. His teaching was remarkable alike for its manner and its matter. As regards the first, it was with such an air of authority and conscious superiority that those who heard Him were astonished, and asked, "Whence hath this Man letters, having never learned?" Whence, indeed! St. Paul had studied the Law under Gamaliel: but where was Jesus taught? No school of prophets, no sect of Pharisees or Sadducees could claim Him as their pupil. And, stranger still, though He taught with such an assumption of authority, He disclaimed all credit for His teaching.

"My doctrine is not Mine, but His that sent Me." "If any man will do His will, he shall know of the doctrine, whether it be of God, or whether I speak from Myself." In short, He claimed to be "a Teacher come from God," sent by God with a message for all mankind. And in this assurance He invited all to come and be His disciples. "Learn of Me, for I am meek and lowly in heart, and ye shall find rest for your souls."

What a wonderful Teacher!

Prof. Wundt, of Leipzig University, in discussing the four imperative motives which make their appeal to the moral consciousness of mankind, and influence life and conduct, tells us that the strongest is that supplied by "the conception of an ideal moral life, together with the emotions and impulses accompanying such a conception."[1] And, in pursuing the subject, he makes the following observations, which, because of their relevancy to the topic before us, I venture to quote.

After speaking of the imperfect approximations to ideal moral perfection exhibited by what we call noble characters, who are "the true intellectual aristocracy," he continues thus—

"But supreme in this aristocracy of morals, as the sun among the planets, shines the ideal character, the moral genius infinitely rarer than any other form that genius ever takes, and brought forth by the spirit of history, perhaps once in hundreds or thousands of years. While the great sum of moral forces works for the present, or at most for the immediate future, the ideal character seems to embody the whole spirit of humanity. It comprehends the entire moral development of the past, and radiates its influence into the remotest distances of the future."[2] Again: "It is doubtless a matter of equal necessity that the ideal character should be the rarest of all endowments, hence to be regarded as *the very manifestation of God on earth* . . . Finally, in those decisive periods when some great change in the conditions of human life, extending beyond the boundaries of a single nation, has brought about a moral crisis, affecting the whole history of the world, and demanding a revolution in moral ideas and theories, then the historical

[1] "Principles of Morality," p. 66.   [2] *Ibid.*, p. 71.

process awaits completion by the power of an ideal character, an ethical genius, whose influence can awaken slumbering impulses to life . . . And the moral ideal, too, has its religious embodiment; indeed, the religious conception is peculiarly effective here, for it represents to each individual *a personal prototype* of the moral conduct of life. In all these ways religion fulfils its function as the great educative force to morality."[1]

These are remarkable words. And as we read them we cannot help asking, how the writer expected his eloquent description of the Ideal Moral Character to be realized?

Could it be that, consciously or unconsciously, he was influenced by the conception of that "Ideal Moral Character" which through the Incarnation, in the Personality and life of Jesus, has been exhibited to mankind?

We are tempted to think so for the following reasons:—

(1) Because the Ideal Moral Character of Jesus, as Christians conceive of it, corresponds in a remarkable manner, and, in some of its more important features, to that ideal character which Prof. Wundt describes and foretells.

(2) Because the temporal crisis and historical conditions, which were to call it forth, were such as prevailed when the Incarnation took place.

Then, too, "the historical process—I would

[1] "Principles of Morality," pp. 71, 72, 73.

prefer to call it the evolutionary process—awaited completion" by the advent of an Ideal Character, an ethical genius.

Then, too, there was "a moral crisis, affecting the whole history of the world, and demanding a revolution in moral ideas and theories." Nor was the demand in vain. In the Ideal Moral Character of Jesus it was answered, and its summons to mankind slumbering in the darkness of ignorance and sin was this: "Awake, thou that sleepest, and arise from the dead, and Christ shall give thee light."

(3) Because, if the ideal character, when at length it should arrive, ought to be regarded as "a veritable manifestation of God upon earth," is not this precisely the view which, according to the teaching of the Spiritual Philosophy, we are asked to take, and do take, of the Ideal Character disclosed to mankind through the Incarnation of Jesus Christ?

(4) Because, judged by results, Wundt's forecast of the work to be accomplished by his ideal character has been fulfilled. Will any one deny that the moral ideal, revealed in the life and Personality of Christ, has been the most educative, elevating force the world has ever seen? Has it not, in truth, "awakened the slumbering impulses of mankind" to a new and better life?

THE CLAIMS OF JESUS

Plato's Raft, and hope of a surer Conveyance

There would be something pathetic in Plato's confession of ignorance on the subject of the soul's immortality, were it not that his words are relieved at last by a ray of hope, mounting almost to a prophetic anticipation of further and more trustworthy guidance. The passage is worth quoting.

"For we ought with respect to these things, either to learn from others how they stand, or to discover them for ourselves; or, if both these are impossible, then, taking the best of human reasonings, and that which is most difficult to be confuted, and embarking on this, as one risks himself on a raft, so to sail through life, unless one could be carried more safely and with less risk on a surer conveyance or some Divine Reason."—"Phaedo," 77.

That which Plato desiderated, that which he almost foresaw, has been realized in the Person of Jesus, the Teacher come from God, the Incarnate Logos, the Divine Reason.

(3) Jesus claimed to be Divine

When asked by one of His disciples, "Lord, show us the Father," He replied, "Believest thou not that I am in the Father, and the Father in Me? He that hath seen Me hath seen the Father" (John xiv. 9, 10).

On another occasion we find Him claiming to

be One with God, "I and the Father are One" (John x. 20).

Again, when His enemies accused Him of being a Samaritan and having a devil, because He made Himself greater than their father Abraham, He calmly replied, "Before Abraham was, *I am.*"

The Claim which Jesus did not make

But while Jesus in these and other passages claimed to be One with the Father, we shall err, I think, if we suppose He claimed equality with God.

He called Himself "the Son of God." And while, as the Son, He shared the attributes of Deity, yet He was careful to guard against the misconception that He claimed equality with the Father. When His disciples were sad at the thought of His departure, He told them they ought rather to rejoice, "because I go unto the Father; for *the Father is greater than I.*" "The words that I say unto you, I speak not of Myself, but the Father abiding in Me doeth His work" (John xiv. 10).

On many occasions we find Him praying to the Father, which is an act of an inferior to a superior being.

On other occasions He speaks of Himself as a servant sent into this world by His Father to do His will and finish His work : " I came not to do Mine own will, but the will of Him that sent Me." "Father, not My will, but Thine be done." " I do nothing of Myself, but as the Father taught Me, I speak these things" (John viii. 28).

He frankly admits there are depths of knowledge in the Divine counsels into which even He was not permitted to penetrate. "But of that day or that hour knoweth no one, not even the angels in heaven, neither the Son, but the Father" (Mark xiii. 32). So, also, there seem to have been limitations of His power: "But to sit on My right hand or on My left hand is not Mine to give" (Mark x. 40).

(4) *Jesus claims all Mankind as His Brethren*

But it is also to be observed, that while Jesus claimed God as His Father, He also claimed all mankind as His brethren. "Inasmuch as ye have done it unto one of the least of these My brethren, ye have done it unto Me" (Matt. xxv. 40).

When, on one occasion, He was told that His mother and His brethren desired to speak with Him, He asked, "Who is My mother or My brethren?" And He looked round about on them who sat about Him, and said, "Behold My mother and My brethren. For whosoever shall do the will of God, the same is My brother and sister and mother" (Mark iii. 33–35).

It is as though He had said to them, "By assuming your nature I have become as one of you. Henceforth I count you all—even the forlorn and outcast, the thief in prison, the sick man on his fever-stricken bed, the hungry, the naked, the destitute—as My brethren, and because they are My brethren they are yours also."[1]

(5) *Jesus claimed to be Free from the taint of Sin*

Such a claim is implicit in the challenge He threw down to His detractors: "Which of you convicteth Me of sin?" (John viii. 46).

He who can pay a ransom for others, must himself need none. And he who can liberate others, must himself be free. But, as we shall see, Jesus claimed to do both, and therefore His claim to be "free from sin," whether true or false, was only what we should expect under the circumstances.

We now come to consider the second class of claims which Jesus made.

B. What Jesus claimed to do

We are left in no doubt on this point. It is clear that Jesus regarded the whole human family as sin-stained, fallen, lost. And the view He took of His mission to this world was to purge away the stains of sin, to raise the fallen and recover the lost.

So He called Himself

---

[1] Doubtless in this claim of Jesus, and this revelation of the Brotherhood of man, we must see the origin of that Christian Socialism, which, as the fulfilment of "the law of Christ," has done more than anything else, perhaps, to ameliorate the condition of mankind.

THE CLAIMS OF JESUS 93

(6) "*The Good Shepherd*"

"The Son of man is come to seek and to save that which was lost" (Luke xix. 10).

"The good Shepherd giveth His life for the sheep" (John x. 11).

(7) *Jesus the Good Physician*

Mankind appeared to Him like patients smitten with a sore disease and doomed to die. So He called Himself the Physician, *Se Hælend*, the Saviour, Who would deliver them from death, and restore them once more to health. "I am come that they might have life, and have it abundantly."[1] "Because I live, ye shall live also."[2] "They that are whole need not a physician, but they that are sick."[3]

(8) *Christus Consolator*

He found men suffering from the effects of sin. Pain and sickness and sorrow were on every side, and the heart of Jesus was touched with Divine compassion for the sufferers.

So He invited all who were in any manner of distress to come to Him, that He might comfort and relieve them.

"Come unto Me, all that travail and are heavy laden, and I will give you rest" (Matt. xi. 29).

[1] John x. 10.   [2] John xiv. 19.   [3] Matt. ix. 12.

(9) *Christus Liberator*

He found them slaves of sin and lust, and He said He had come to set them free.

"Ye shall know the truth, and the truth shall make you free." "If the Son shall make you free, ye shall be free indeed" (John viii. 32, 36).

(10) *Christus Redemptor*

"The Son of man came not to be ministered unto, but to minister, and to give His life a ransom for many" (Mark x. 45).

In these words Jesus makes a double claim. First, that He had come as a servant to minister to others. Secondly, to give up His life as the redemption money [1] for the release of the captives.

Whatever interpretation we may put upon this mysterious claim of Jesus "to give His life a ransom for many," it seems to summarize the great objects of the Incarnation. By this supreme act of loving and voluntary self-sacrifice He claims to make a reconciliation or at-one-ment between God and man, between those, in short, whom sin—the Separator—had parted asunder.

This claim of Jesus, however, is one of such cardinal importance in connection with the Incarnation, and, moreover, occupies such a prominent position in the Spiritual Philosophy, that its

---

[1] The Greek word rendered "ransom" in the text (*lytron*) denotes the price to be paid for the release of a prisoner.

more careful and detailed consideration must be reserved to a subsequent chapter.

(11) *Christus Rex: the Kingdom of Heaven*

The mission of Jesus was not to be limited to this present sphere of earthly temporal life. He claimed to be a King; to have come to found a kingdom, but a kingdom "not of this world." This claim He placed in the forefront of His preaching, "Repent ye, for the kingdom of heaven is at hand." How many of His parables were specially intended to instruct His hearers in the nature of this kingdom, I need not point out. When He taught His disciples to pray, this was one of the foremost petitions: "Thy kingdom come." And when Pilate asked Him, "Art Thou a King, then?" He did not deny it, but replied, "Thou sayest that I am King." And further than this, before He went away He laid it as a solemn obligation on His Apostles that they too should carry on His kingly mission, and go forth into all the world, and preach the Gospel of the kingdom.[1]

---

[1] Prof. Eucken regards this claim of Jesus to found a kingdom as one of paramount importance. "If," he says, "Jesus stands so far above all mere enthusiasts and revolutionaries the difference is in the content of the newly proclaimed kingdom, For this content consists in the most intimate fellowship with God, the blessedness arising from such fellowship, and the inseparable union of trust in God with love for men. . . . Here a new life wells up with new aims and powers, a life that represents impressively to humanity a lofty and imperishable ideal, a life which unites with a great expectation

THE CLAIMS OF JESUS IN REGARD TO HIS FUTURE WORK

In addition to all that Jesus claimed to do in fulfilment of His earthly mission and in the course of His ministry, He clearly intimated that His work would still be incomplete.

For that work was to bring mankind into loving conscious union and communion with God. But this meant a spiritual transformation, and required a spiritual agency. Such an agency was necessary in order to produce a real saving conviction of the truth and teaching of Jesus in the hearts of His followers. Hence He claimed to be

(12) *Christus Intercessor*

"I will pray the Father, and He shall give you another Comforter, even the Spirit of Truth" (John xiv. 16). "Neither pray I for these alone, but for them also who shall believe on Me through their word" (John xiv. 20).

And as He hung upon the cross, His first words were words of intercession for His murderers: "Father, forgive them; for they know not what they do."

---

and hope a veritable transfiguration of the present. Seen from the point of view of this concept, the kingdom of heaven is already present in the souls of men."—Prof. Eucken's "The Problem of Human Life," p. 153 ff.

THE CLAIMS OF JESUS

Such, then, were some of the more important claims which were made on behalf of Jesus, either by His followers to whom we are indebted for the Gospel records of His life and ministry, or by Himself. I have mentioned them, not with the view of discussing their veracity, but because, in the first place, they make up the picture and objective background of the percept of the Incarnation. Secondly, because, whether true or false, they form the index of the inner consciousness of Jesus, and therefore of His Personality. And thirdly, because they are the root of those *concepts* which, taken as a whole, constitute that form of religious belief we call Christianity, and so have given rise to the highest development and enrichment of the human psychè, or soul, namely, *Spiritual Consciousness*.

The consciousness of Jesus demands more than a passing notice, and will, therefore, form the subject of the next chapter.

CHAPTER IX

SPIRITUAL CONSCIOUSNESS—*continued*

The truth of the Incarnation, as witnessed by the consciousness of Jesus—The standing Miracle of all time—The picture of Jesus—Who painted this picture?—Conclusions.

THE CONSCIOUSNESS OF JESUS

BEFORE passing to the consideration of those concepts to which, through apperception, the percept of the Incarnation gives rise, I will ask my readers to pause a few moments, and reflect on the consciousness of Jesus as revealed by the astonishing claims He made. I think we might call it—

THE STANDING MIRACLE OF ALL TIME

The objection which has been felt and urged by many against the acceptance of the Gospel story is that it renders necessary a belief in miracles. Miracles, they say, are contrary to experience. "We never saw one, and we hold that they cannot happen, and no evidence is sufficient to convince us that they ever did."

Let me ask those who adopt this line of

SPIRITUAL CONSCIOUSNESS

argument to turn their thoughts for a moment to the consciousness of Jesus.

Here, in the consciousness of Jesus, we are confronted with a psychological fact, or a spiritual phenomenon, if you will, of paramount importance; a fact which cannot be denied, but yet of such a marvellous and transcendent nature that no miracle which Jesus is ever said to have wrought can for a moment compare with it. It was and must ever remain the standing miracle of all time.

It was contrary to experience; for never before nor since has such a phenomenon occurred. And yet it was experienced: "And we beheld His glory, the glory as of the Only-begotten of the Father, full of grace and truth" (John i. 14). "That which we have heard, that which we have seen with our eyes, that which we beheld, and our hands handled, concerning the Word of life . . . declare we unto you also" (1 John i. 1-3).

How will the objectors to all miracles meet this difficulty? How, in other words, will they explain away this cardinal miracle of the consciousness of Jesus?

Assuming, as I suppose will be generally admitted, that Jesus did really make the claims He is said to have done, there seem to be four, and only four, suppositions by which they may be accounted for.

(1) Either, that He was a religious fanatic, Whose zeal so wrought upon His imagination

that He persuaded Himself that He was what He claimed to be.

(2) That He was a wilful impostor, and that, for some reason not explained, He put forth all these extraordinary claims, well knowing them to be false.

(3) That Jesus Himself never made these claims, but that they were invented and attributed to Him long after His death, either consciously or unconsciously, in order to invest Him with a Divine nature and attributes, and so secure the spread of His religion. This hypothesis was first put forth, I believe, by the German Professor, Dr. Strauss, and goes by the name of *the Mythical Theory*.

(4) That Jesus was what He claimed to be; that His consciousness, as revealed by His claims, was not the result of a disordered or over-wrought imagination, still less of intentional fraud and imposition, but attributable only to the presence of the Deity within Him.

The first two of these hypotheses are so wildly improbable, that I cannot imagine any sane person undertaking to defend them. The third, the mythical hypothesis, will not bear examination, for the simple reason that there is not an atom of evidence to show that the immediate followers of Jesus preached any other Gospel than that which has been persistently handed down through the Catholic Church to the present day, a Gospel not of a book, but of a Person, a Gospel based on the truth of two stupendous miracles—the Incarnation and the Resurrection.

If this be so, then the only remaining theory is the last; namely, that the consciousness of Jesus was in truth and reality the consciousness of a Divine Personality, *i.e.* the Logos, or Word of God.

The Picture of Jesus

And now let us try to envisage the portrait of Jesus as presented to us in the Gospel records, clothed in all the attributes He claimed. What a picture we shall have! Remember, too, that the evidence those claims afford to the character and inner consciousness of Jesus is of the cumulative order. We may not single out this or that, and exclude the rest. Let us put all these claims together, and imagine them as the moral and spiritual characteristics of the one Personality of Jesus.

We may not say, for example, "We admire the beautiful character of Jesus, His gentleness, His goodness, His altruism. We revere Him as a great Moral Teacher, and we think men would do well to follow His example. But more than this we cannot admit. The best of men He may have been, but to His claim to be Divine we must respectfully demur. His claim to work miracles we can in no wise allow, for miracles are contrary to our experience, and therefore nothing can persuade us that they ever take place."

But is this spirit of eclecticism justified in the case before us? Are we free to pick out just those claims which seem to us admissible, and reject the rest? Would it not be both to destroy the integrity of His character, and the consistency of His teaching? Would it not be to set up another Jesus, divested of the essential features which characterize the Jesus of the Gospels—the only Jesus with Whom history and experience have made us acquainted? And so, if we would present to our mind's eye a faithful picture of Jesus, it must be the Jesus Whom we know, the Jesus Who "went about doing good," and "healing all manner of sickness and all manner of disease among the people."

And when we have succeeded in presenting to our minds the Jesus of the Gospels, what a wonderful, what an arresting picture we shall have! Let us pause a moment in silent contemplation, and try to understand something of its meaning.

The miraculous element in Christianity has sometimes been regarded as its weakest point, and a drawback and obstacle to its acceptance. But here in this portrait of Jesus, you have drawn, have you not, a miracle before your eyes which far transcends all other miracles—a miracle which no ingenuity can explain away, and no subtle argument can destroy?

Who painted this Picture?

Who amongst the disciples of Jesus could have conceived or painted such a picture? Could St. John, or Peter, or Paul have done it? Did any of them claim to have done it? No. They, like ourselves, were but spectators. They, too, were convinced of its truth and entranced by its beauty and sublimity. From it they drew their inspiration; for it they gladly faced persecution and death; and all they did was to try and exhibit it to the world, that others might be captivated by its truth and loveliness.

If Jesus did not make these claims Himself, we certainly have a right to ask, "Who made them for Him?" And if no answer is forthcoming, we seem justified in assuming that He Himself did so.

"Whence hath this Man this wisdom and these mighty works?" The question is one which we too are bound to face. Think of the mighty sweep of His outlook on mankind; the breadth of His love and the depth of His sympathy; the gentleness and serenity of His disposition; the beauty, and yet the severity, of His moral teaching; His stern denunciation of sin, coupled as it was with tenderest love for the sinner; the sublimity of His teaching about God, and His entire submission to His will.

These are a few, and only a few, of the features

which invest the picture of Jesus with its indescribable loveliness, its impressive grandeur, its constraining power.

Conclusions

The following, then, are the conclusions to which the treatment of our subject, according to the principles of the Spiritual Philosophy, seem to bring us:—

(1) That we have in the Incarnation, and all it connotes, a further, and perhaps a final, manifestation of God—of the Infinite in terms of the finite.

(2) That this manifestation is in accordance with, and analogous to, all previous manifestations, both as to method, means, and end. For,

(*a*) It is evolutionary.

(*b*) It is through the activity of the same Divine agencies: the Logos, or Word, and the Hokmah, or life-giving Spirit of wisdom.

(3) Its end is the completion, or consummation, of that purpose which has been in progress from the first, the gradual approach of the creature to the Creator, the reunion of life in its highest form—the personal self-conscious soul of man—with its parent Spirit, God.

Such, then, is the new environment, which through the Incarnation has been created for mankind. Here in the exhibition of the ideal moral character of Jesus we have the last and noblest percept. But the same rule holds good as before. The percept must by the power of apperception be transmuted into the concept—the Divine idea—that love is the law of the highest life, the very fulfilment of all law, and that, therefore, which, when responded to, brings the human into harmony with the Divine.

"A fire-mist and a planet,
A crystal and a cell,
A jelly-fish and a saurian,
And a cave where the Cave-men dwell;
Then a sense of law and beauty,
And a face turned from the clod :—
Some call it *Evolution*,
And others call it *God*.

"A haze in the far horizon,
The infinite tender sky,
The ripe rich tint of the corn-fields,
And the wild geese sailing high,
And all over upland and lowland
The charm of the golden rod :—
Some of us call it *Autumn*,
And others call it *God*.

"Like tides on a crescent sea-beach
When the moon is new and thin,
Into our hearts high yearnings
Come welling and surging in—
Come from the mystic ocean
Whose rim no foot hath trod :—
Some of us call it *Longing*,
And others call it *God*.

"A picket frozen on duty,
A mother starved for her brood,
Socrates drinking the hemlock,
And Jesus on the rood;

And millions who, humble and faithful,
The strait hard pathway trod:—
Some call it *Consecration*,
And others call it *God*."[1]

---

[1] The author of these beautiful lines is W. H. Carruth, German Professor, Kansas University.

CHAPTER X

SPIRITUAL CONSCIOUSNESS—*continued*

Primary concept arising from the Incarnation—Love, the Norm of the highest life, displayed in the Atonement.

MY object in this chapter is to show that the primary concept to which the Incarnation gives rise is Love, as the Norm[1] of the highest life; and secondly, that the doctrine of the Atonement, as set forth in the Gospel records, is the proof of it.

By Atonement (at-one-ment) we understand reconciliation, in the special sense of restoring terms of peace and amity between two persons, God and man, who had previously been alienated. And, therefore, it means, necessarily, in the second place, the removal of that which had caused the alienation and separation. But sin is the separator, the cause of the discord and alienation. Therefore, sin must, somehow, be got rid of. And this is just what Jesus came to do—" to put away sin by the sacrifice of Himself."

Of the claims which Jesus made for Himself none were more astonishing and significant than those which set forth the great purpose for which He said He had come into the world.

---

[1] *I.e.* the pattern or type.

"The Son of Man came to seek and to save that which was lost" (Luke xix. 10).

Here He compares mankind to sheep which have wandered far off into the wilderness, have lost their way, and are in danger of perishing; and He called Himself the Good Shepherd, whose object it was to seek out the lost sheep and bring them back to the fold.

On another occasion we find Him saying, "The Son of man came not to be ministered unto, but to minister, and to give His life a ransom for many" (Mark x. 45; Matt. xx. 28).

Here the purpose for which He came into the world is stated in more specific terms—to pay with His life-blood the ransom or redemption money which must be paid for the release of a captive taken in war, or the emancipation of a slave.

From these utterances of Jesus we may gather what was His own conception of the work He came to perform—the work which He said again and again His Father had given Him to do.

To put it briefly, it was the work of atonement and reconciliation, the work of bringing mankind back again to God as their heavenly Father, by removing the causes of their previous estrangement, and so effecting a reconciliation between them.[1]

---

[1] "Jesus, by His disclosure of the beauty of the Divine character of holiness and love—each explanatory of the other—so set forth the spiritual principle of morality that it is seen to be man's true expression of himself, that wherein he finds his true freedom. He

The purpose of the Atonement, then, was to render possible and provide the means for bringing mankind into union and communion with God. And further, it was through suffering and death that all this was to be accomplished. How are we to understand this? Why was it necessary? Let us look into this point more closely.

But here it behoves us to be on our guard against certain misconceptions.

Did God need any sacrifice to render Him propitious to mankind? Or can we imagine that the sufferings and death of His beloved Son were pleasing to Him as constituting such a sacrifice of propitiation?

Neither of these suppositions, I venture to think, can be entertained. As regards the first, namely, that God required a sacrifice to render Him propitious to mankind, such a view seems both unscriptural and repugnant to our ideas of the goodness of God. How can such a view be reconciled with the plain words of Jesus Himself, "God so loved the world, that He gave His only-begotten Son, that whosoever believeth on Him should not perish, but have everlasting life"?

From which we must infer that, whatever

gave Himself, so that the Divine life might belong to man in a sense in which it had not previously been his. He took humanity to Himself, that He might spiritualize it. And the condition for the giving of His life for mankind was, in the wisdom and providence of God, the cross which Christ endured for the joy that was set before Him of regenerating humanity "—Dr. Askwith's "Sin and the Need of Atonement," p. 218, *Cambridge Theological Essays*, p. 218.

other purpose was to be accomplished by the Incarnation and the Atonement, it was not to propitiate an angry God in favour of mankind, because already He loved them and deemed no sacrifice too great to win them back to Himself. And both the Incarnation and the Atonement were but the manifestations of Divine love.

The second supposition,—that the sufferings of Jesus were in themselves pleasing to God,—seems equally untenable; and that for a similar reason.

THE VICARIOUS OR SUBSTITUTIONAL VIEW

Closely akin to this latter misconception of the sufferings of Jesus, is that which has been called the vicarious or substitutional view.

According to this view, the sufferings and death of Christ have themselves been regarded as the Atonement. Christ by His death on the cross bore the penalty of human sin, and rendered it possible for God to forgive the sinner. The sufferings of the innocent availed for the clearing of the guilty. But against this way of regarding the matter, as Dr. Askwith truly remarks,[1] there has been a strong protest and reaction, as doing violence even to our human ideas of justice.[2]

[1] "Sin and the Need of Atonement," *Camb. Theological Essays.*

[2] I know there are texts, not a few, which may be cited which seem to favour the substitutional and vicarious view, such, for example, as 1 Pet. iii. 18, "For Christ also hath once suffered for sins, the just for the unjust"; Tit. ii. 14, "Who gave Himself for us"; and many others of a similar nature. But in all cases the preposition in

The same writer goes on to ask, "If God only forgives sin when the penalty has been borne, is there such a thing as Divine forgiveness at all?" I remember once seeing a terrible picture, symbolical of the Atonement, in one of the Continental churches, I forget which, in which God was represented as an angry father, armed with a spear which he was about to hurl at his fugitive son. A more shocking travesty of the Christian doctrine of the Incarnation it would be impossible to imagine.

Shall we say, then, that the Atonement which Christ made by His sufferings and death had no sacrificial and propitiatory efficacy in the sight of God? Certainly not. The mere fact that Jesus was a son of man as well as the Son of God, human as well as Divine, forbids us to think so. As the Representative of Humanity, as the Type of a new Creation, He offered His sacrifice to God, and as such God was pleased to accept it. We may well believe, therefore, that it may have effected a change, not in the love of the Father towards mankind, which was capable neither of change nor increase, but in His sentiment towards a race whom sin had corrupted and alienated, but were no longer to be regarded as in rebellion against Him.[1]

Greek is (ὑπὲρ) "in behalf of" not (ἀντί) "instead of," which seems conclusive against the substitutional view pure and simple.

[1] St. Paul enlarges on this aspect of the Atonement in Rom. v. 8-19.

All this must be frankly and thankfully admitted.

But here the mystical aspect of the Atonement comes into view—an aspect into which neither time nor space permits me to enter in detail. Christ ever taught His disciples they must enter into a mystical union with Himself if they wished to share the benefits of His Incarnation and Atonement. "Abide in Me, and I in you: as the branch cannot bear fruit except it abide in the vine, no more can ye except ye abide in Me; for apart from Me ye can do nothing."

It is, then, through being brought into mystical union with Christ that we come within the pale of His Atonement, and are "accepted in the Beloved."

"In Him dwelleth all the fulness of the Godhead bodily," and "We too are complete in Him," by virtue of His indwelling in us. This was what St. Paul felt and expressed when he said, "I am crucified with Christ; nevertheless, I live: yet, not I, but Christ liveth in me" (Gal. ii. 20).

But if the sufferings of Jesus had in themselves no intrinsic value in the sight of God; and if He did not suffer ($ἀντί$) instead of us, but only ($ὑπέρ$) in our behalf, the question may naturally be asked, Why was it necessary He should have suffered at all? Why could Jesus, as the

Captain of man's salvation, only be "made perfect through sufferings" (Heb. ii. 10)?

The answer is one which involves the mystery of evil. The nature of the case, the conditions under which the At-one-ment had to be made, could not but entail suffering on the part of Him Who made it. A moment's consideration will show this.

If there be, as we cannot doubt, a real antithesis and antagonism between good and evil in the world, and if in the sphere of human life this antithesis and antagonism is actively displayed, it follows, as a necessary consequence, that any one, God or man, who should adventure himself into this arena of strife as the champion of goodness and truth, must incur for himself a life of suffering. But this is just what Jesus did, knowingly and voluntarily. He came, as He said, "to bear witness to the truth"; He entered the lists to wage a deadly warfare against sin and evil, as the Champion of goodness and truth. Hence it was inevitable, from the nature of the case, that He should be "a Man of sorrows and acquainted with grief"; that, if He was a true Messiah, sent by God, He should be "the suffering Servant of Jehovah."

He came as the great Emancipator to deliver mankind from the thraldom of sin to follow righteousness; to exhibit to the world the uplifting spectacle of loving self-sacrifice on behalf of others.

It was nothing short of a Divine revelation, "a very manifestation," to use the words of Prof. Wundt, "of God upon earth." But chief above all it was intended to teach us that "love is the Norm of the highest life," because it is the very life of God.

Response

This is the new environment, which through the Incarnation and Atonement has been created for mankind. But again, as we said before, there must be response. And what that response should be, I cannot summarize better than in the words of two of the Master's most devoted followers—

"Let this mind be in you, which was also in Christ Jesus" (Phil. ii. 5).

"Beloved, let us love one another; for love is of God: and every one that loveth is born of God, and knoweth God. He that loveth not, knoweth not God; for God is love" (1 John iv. 7).

CHAPTER XI

SPIRITUAL CONSCIOUSNESS—*continued*

Some secondary concepts arising from the percept of the Incarnation; (1) The Personality and Fatherhood of God; (2) The brotherhood of man, and Christian Socialism.

DOUBTLESS there are a considerable number of secondary concepts to which the percept of the Incarnation gives rise. My remarks, however, in this chapter must be limited to two of them, which seem to me of paramount importance. They are—
  (1) The Personality and Fatherhood of God.
  (2) The Brotherhood of Man.

(1) THE PERSONALITY AND FATHERHOOD OF GOD

The first of these springs from the persistent claims and teaching of Jesus as to His relation to God. In order to enable His disciples to understand in some measure the nature of this relationship, and out of condescension to their ignorance and finite understanding, He made use of the human relationship of fatherhood.

He ever called and addressed God as His Father; *e.g.*: "So shall My heavenly Father do also unto you," etc. He spoke of Him as no metaphysical abstraction of Whom not even "being" could be predicated (Plotinus); no absolute undifferentiated Something, which transcends both description and imagination; but as a Personal Spirit, between Whom and His own self-conscious Personality intercourse and communion were possible. "No man hath seen God at any time," says the Apostle John. But he adds, "The Only-begotten Son, Who is in the bosom of the Father, He hath declared Him" (John i. 18). Which means I take it, that the Personality of the Son reveals the Personality of the Father, and assists us in realizing that Personality.

I was talking to a friend some time ago, when our conversation turned on this very subject of the Personality of God. "Do you know," he said, "I am sometimes tempted to doubt the truth of this doctrine; and whether, after all, it may not be a projection on the field of imagination of the idea or image of our own personality. I am not sure if the doctrine of the Supreme Being propounded by Plotinus, of an abstract impersonal essence, presents greater difficulty."

It may be that others have experienced a similar doubt and difficulty. If so, I would suggest to them, as I did to my friend, that, if they would approach the subject from the side of the Incarnation, they would probably find their difficulty removed. Doubtless it is not easy to realize the existence of God as a Personal Father. But, if we can accept the Divine Personality of the Son as it is exhibited to us in the Gospel records, it seems to me we ought not to find much difficulty in realizing the Divine Personality of the Father. For without the Father there can be no Son, and, in that case, both the character and claims of Jesus fall to the ground.

But not only did Jesus make use of the figure of fatherhood to illustrate the nature of His own relationship to God, He taught men that they, too, may call God their Father. Did He turn their thoughts to the Universe around them, or the operations of Nature, to the rising and setting of the sun, the clothing of the lilies, the feeding of the ravens—"all these," He said, "are the works of your heavenly Father."

"Be ye, therefore, perfect, even as your Father, Who is in heaven, is perfect."

When His disciples came to Him with the request, "Lord, teach us to pray," how did He tell them to address God? Not as the Eternal, the Infinite, the Absolute, but simply as "our Father."

And when, on the morning of the Resurrection, the penitent Magdalene, in her overpowering joy, would have clasped His feet, He forbade her, saying, "Touch Me not, for I am not yet ascended unto *My* Father . . . and *your* Father and to *My* God and *your* God."

Not this time "our Father" and "our God," but "yours" and "Mine"; so teaching us that, though God was the Father of both, His own relation to God as His Father was different from ours.

He was the Son of God by eternal generation: "Begotten of the Father before all worlds." We are sons of God only in time, and by gradual evolution and the infusion of the Holy Spirit. He was "the First-born of every creature," and "in Him dwelleth all the fulness of the Godhead bodily." We follow at an infinite distance behind; and in us the Divine image, whatever it may have been originally, has been blurred and mutilated by sin.

He was One with the Father from the beginning; we can only hope to become so by the final victory over sin, and by the renewing influence of the Holy Spirit.

"The Voice of God's Creation found me
  Perplex'd midst hope and fear,
For though His sunshine flash'd around me,
  His storms at times drew near:
    And I said—
Oh! that I knew where He abideth!
  For doubts beset our lot,
And lo! His glorious face He hideth,
  And men perceive it not!
    .   .   .   .   .
"It was the Voice of Revelation
  That met my utmost need:
The wondrous message of salvation
  Was joy and peace indeed:

SPIRITUAL CONSCIOUSNESS

> And I said—
> Oh! how I love the sacred pages
> From which such tidings flow,
> As monarchs, patriarchs, poets, sages,
> Have long'd in vain to know!
>
> "For now is life a lucid story,
> And death a rest in Him,
> And all is bathed in light and glory
> That once was dark or dim.
> And I said—
> O Thou Who dost my soul deliver,
> And all its hopes uplift;
> Give me a tongue to praise the Giver,
> A heart to prize the gift."
> (Hymns A. & M. 530.)

(2) THE BROTHERHOOD OF MAN

This concept may be regarded as an inferential concept from that of the Fatherhood of God. For all those who have a common Father must needs also be brethren. But the concept derives its origin even more directly from the Incarnation. If the Son of God became true Man, and as such claimed to be the Brother of all,[1] then again all men are brethren. So far as men can truly call Jesus Brother, so far will they recognize the relation of brotherhood into which by the Incarnation they have been brought.

Here again we have an instance of the ethical value of the Incarnation, and for this reason the concept of Brotherhood has ever occupied a prominent place and exercised a paramount

---

[1] Cf. "Inasmuch as ye have done it unto one of the least of these My brethren, ye have done it unto Me" (Matt. xxv. 40).

influence in Christian ethics. "Love as brethren. Be pitiful, be courteous," is to be the rule of Christian conduct. The follower of Jesus must ever be a Christian Socialist. "Let no man seek his own," says St. Paul, "but every man another's wealth." And St. John goes even further, and makes the practical display of this concept the very test of the new life : " By this we know that we have passed from death unto life, because we love the brethren."

At the same time, we cannot disguise from ourselves the fact that there is a Socialism of a very different character from that which found its origin in the idea of Christian brotherhood. The socialistic trend of thought and activity was, perhaps, never more pronounced and insistent than it is at the present time; so much so that it threatens to eclipse both philosophy and religion. Nay, more than this, we see it arrogating to itself the very name of religion. And humanity, according to the late August Comte, is itself the highest and only worthy object of worship for mankind. But I must not enlarge on this aspect of Socialism here. I only refer to it to show that, while Christian Socialism is one of the most beautiful concepts to which the Incarnation has given rise, there is a Socialism which is only a travesty and perversion of it, and subversive alike both of philosophy and religion in the truer meaning of those words.

CHAPTER XII

PERCEPT V.—THE HOLY SPIRIT

Rival spiritualistic theories: (I.) the Pluralistic; (II.) the Monistic or Unitary—The Holy Spirit in the Old and New Testament Scriptures: (*a*) In the Old Testament; (*b*) In the New Testament—Primary concept: Holiness—Secondary concept: The dignity of the body.

BEFORE proceeding to the consideration of the percept of the Holy Spirit, as we believe it to have been and to be specially manifested in and through the Incarnation, it seems desirable briefly to review the two rival theories of spiritualism which at the present time divide the philosophic world.[1]

I. THE PLURALISTIC THEORY

These two theories are (1) the Pluralistic and (2) the Unitary or Monistic theories. According to the former, the ultimate Reality may be the sum-total of an infinite number of individual spirits, or units, which form together a community or commonwealth, but which lack any head or

---

[1] "The alternative between Pluralism and Monism," says the late Prof. James, "is the most frequent of all the dilemmas of philosophy." —"Some Problems," p. 114.

animating, controlling principle, and in which there is no room for consciousness, except such as is found in each individual unit.

Dr. McTaggart, who stands as the champion of this theory, holds "that the Absolute is not a person, not conscious, not a monistic being for itself in a central way, but a Divine city, a spiritual college, a union in which the unity is resident in the members and rises to consciousness only in them."[1]

The individual units may possess consciousness, they may form a system, they may be infinite in number, but after all they are discrete particles, so to speak. They are like a body without a head; and apparently there is no nexus binding them together, correlating them, and providing the means of interaction. Except that consciousness exists in each independent member, it exists nowhere in the universe beside.

II. The Monistic or Unitary Theory

The second theory of spiritualism is the Monistic or Unitary theory, and the leading tenets are briefly these—

(1) There is one universal Monistic Spirit of Consciousness.

(2) All finite spirits are derivative, and created

---

[1] Cf. Dr. Caldecott, on "The Being of God," *Camb. Essays*, p. 136. Pluralism as thus conceived seems to be a conflation of the philosophies of Plotinus, Hegel, and Comte.

PERCEPT V.—THE HOLY SPIRIT

in the sense of proceeding from the Divine Universal Spirit. They are streams or rills of consciousness, issuing from the one and only Source of all consciousness, which is God.

Against the theory of pluralistic spiritualism there are several serious objections.

(1) In the first place, there is the difficulty of conceiving how such an infinite congeries of independent isolated spirits could come into existence at all. Are they self-created out of nothing? for clearly they can have no Creator. But if so, we must reverse the dictum, *Ex nihilo nihil fit.*

(2) If the ultimate reality consists only in an infinity of finite units, this sort of infinity fails to meet the demand of our conscious reason for an infinity not only of number, but of magnitude and power.

But we may go even a step further. For the soul of man, as representing the latest product and highest value of the Evolutionary Process, with all its faculties and emotions of love and aspiration, requires for its satisfaction, and as the ultimate and objective reality, not only a being corresponding to itself, but infinite also in goodness, truth, and love.[1]

---

[1] " We need infinity in connection with every ultimate category of our spiritual life. For the category of being we must have a unity of centre as well as a unity of system; a central Spirit from which all finite spirits issue as differentiations, in which they continue, and through which alone they can enter into system at all. Apart from

(3) But perhaps the strongest argument against pluralistic spiritualism is this, namely, that it does not harmonize with our experience of the nature and tendency of Creative Evolution.

If there is one fact that Evolution impresses on us more than another, it is that the process is unitary and monistic. We see that there have been an infinite number of forces at work—physical, mental, psychical; but they have all been co-operant factors. They are all co-ordinated as means to one end—the gradual development of conscious psychic spiritual intelligences, fitted for union and communion with each other, and with the one Source of all consciousness and intelligence which is God.

Conscious intelligence is the one common characteristic which is impressed on the whole system of Creative Evolution. The consciousness exhibited by the lower forms of life is vastly inferior to that displayed by the reasonable self-conscious personality of man; and yet they are rungs on the same ladder, links in the one unbroken chain of psychical development. But who would dream of splitting consciousness into sections? We are bound to believe that every form and grade of consciousness is the offshoot from one and the same Source and Centre of all

this central personality, the unity of being exists only for the constituent members, and is therefore only an infinite repetition of ideas of a system."—"Philosophy and the Being of God," by Dr. A. Caldecott, *Camb. Essays*, p. 137.

PERCEPT V.—THE HOLY SPIRIT

consciousness, the Holy Spirit of wisdom, "which sweetly ordereth all things," and "in Whom we live, and move, and have our being."

If this be so, the doctrine of pluralistic spiritualism must be rejected as incompatible with our experience of Creative Evolution.

THE HOLY SPIRIT IN THE OLD AND NEW TESTAMENT SCRIPTURES

The witness of the Old Testament Scriptures, canonical and uncanonical, to the existence, work, and office of the Holy Spirit, has already come under review in my last book, "Some Thoughts on God." It seems unnecessary, therefore, to go over the same ground again.

(a) IN THE OLD TESTAMENT

At the time of the Incarnation the doctrine of the Holy Spirit, or as He is called in the Sapiential Literature, the Hokmah, or Spirit of Divine wisdom, had become one of the recognized and permanent articles of Jewish belief. When the Baptist, referring to Jesus, said, "There standeth One among you, Whom ye know not: He shall baptize you with the Holy Ghost and with fire," there was no need for him to explain Who this Holy Ghost was. And when Jesus told Nicodemus, "Except a man be born of water and of the Spirit, he cannot enter into the kingdom of God" (John iii. 5), it was not the reference to the Spirit that perplexed him, but the strange doctrine of the new birth. This means that the doctrine of the Holy Spirit, as held and taught by the Jewish Church, was accepted by the founders of the Christian religion, and by them incorporated into the body of the Christian Faith.

"The experience of the primitive Church," says Dr. Swete, "was but a continuation and enlargement of the experience of the Church of Israel, which is expressed in the Old Testament. The New Testament doctrine of the Spirit begins where the Old Testament doctrine breaks off."[1]

(b) IN THE NEW TESTAMENT

But in the diagram of psychic Evolution No. 2, Percept V., the Holy Spirit is used in a somewhat expanded sense as embracing, not only the Old Testament percept, but that further, fuller manifestation and sphere of activity it received in connection with the Incarnation.

In the Gospel records the Holy Spirit is presented to us under a twofold aspect. First, He is exhibited as a conspiring and co-operating Agent with the Logos in effecting the Incarnation.[2] Secondly, as a personal Energy, necessary

[1] "The Holy Spirit in the New Testament," p. 6.

[2] Cf. "The Holy Ghost shall come upon thee, and the power of the Most High shall overshadow thee: therefore also that Holy Thing that shall be born of thee shall be called holy, the Son of God" (Luke i. 35).

PERCEPT V.—THE HOLY SPIRIT

to the carrying on and completion of the work of Christ. Christ came as Redeemer, Teacher, Exemplar; and as such His work was exterior to man. But the work of the Holy Spirit was to be within man—to quicken in him a new spiritual life.

PRIMARY CONCEPT: HOLINESS

Thus the concept of the Holy Spirit is again, as before in the physical world, that of the Lifegiver. But this time, not the animal or psychic life, but that spiritual life which is the life of holiness and love, and, therefore, the life of God Himself.

The Holy Spirit, then, is to find His sphere of action in those innermost recesses of man's spiritual nature where thought and sentiment and aspiration take their rise.

His work is to enlighten the conscience; to beget a sense of the beauty of holiness; to stimulate and strengthen the will; to kindle and purify the affections; to bring home with saving force and conviction the truths that Jesus taught. "He shall bring to your mind all things whatsoever I have said unto you." "He shall take of Mine, and shall show it unto you."

As by the co-operation of the Holy Spirit, the Word became flesh and dwelt amongst us, so by the co-operation of the same two Agents, the

Incarnation, in a certain true and real, though spiritual, sense, is extended so as to embrace all mankind. Christ, by the indwelling Spirit, takes up His abode in the hearts of those who will receive Him. And thus was the promise to be fulfilled: "I will not leave you comfortless: I will come unto you."

Thus is man to become "a habitation of God through the Spirit."[1] "A partaker of the Divine Nature."[2]

Secondary Concept of the Holy Spirit: the Worth and Dignity of the Body

The work of the Holy Spirit is not exhausted in its quickening, renewing, and sanctifying influence on the soul. The body, too, is to feel and respond to that influence. It is true the flesh and spirit are regarded by St. Paul as antagonistic principles (Gal. v. 16-24; vi. 8); "as irreconcilable enemies engaged in a warfare which continues to the end of life."[3] It is true that *the flesh* represents the lower animal side of human nature, and that the work of the Spirit is to strengthen the higher spiritual side in its struggle with the proclivities and temptations arising from the lower sensual side. But in saying this, we have not said all. Both flesh

---

[1] Eph. ii. 22.
[2] 2 Pet. i. 4.
[3] Dr. Swete, "The Holy Spirit in the New Testament," p. 394.

PERCEPT V.—THE HOLY SPIRIT

and spirit are component elements of human nature, and both are to become the subjects of the Holy Spirit's sanctifying, purifying influence. Our *bodies* are to become "temples of the Holy Ghost." We are to "yield our members as instruments of righteousness." We are to glorify God in our bodies as well as our spirits, for both belong to God.

And here it is that the Spiritual Philosophy presents so marked a contrast to those religious systems, such as Buddhism, in which the physical side of human nature is regarded as the source of all sin and misery, and therefore a thing to be despised and got rid of as soon as possible.

But this concept of the worth and dignity of the body brings us face to face with another problem, namely, the place of death in evolution. This subject, however, is one of such great interest and importance, that it seems desirable to devote a separate chapter to its discussion.

"THE more thoroughly we comprehend the process of evolution, the more profoundly shall we feel that to deny the immortality of the soul is to rob the whole process of its meaning. Man is a fruit which it needed all that went before to ripen. He is the last and greatest achievement of evolution. To suppose that what has been evolved at such a cost will suddenly collapse, is to suppose that the whole scheme of things is self-stultifying. It is to convert the whole drama of Creation into an imbecile and drivelling farce."—Dr. Momerie, "Immortality," p. 39.

CHAPTER XIII

THE SURVIVAL OF MAN

I. The argument from faith in the Incarnation—II. The argument from Evolution—The place of death in Evolution—Two theories of cerebral function in relation to thought: (a) The Production theory—(b) The Transmission theory—The Pauline view—III. The argument from spiritual manifestations and psychical research.

THERE are two points of view from which the subject of the survival of man after death may be regarded.

The first is that of the Incarnation; the second is that of Evolution. Both views will afford arguments in favour of the survival of man, though they differ in kind.

The argument derived from the Incarnation we may call the argument from faith. That derived from Evolution is the argument from inference and probability.

I. THE ARGUMENT FROM FAITH

If we can accept the doctrine of the Incarnation, and what it connotes, that Jesus was perfect God as well as perfect Man—the Teacher come from God—then that belief carries with it the assurance of a future life for body and soul after death : " Because I live, ye shall live also." "The hour cometh, when all that are in their graves shall hear the voice of the Son of man, and shall come forth," etc. There will be a resurrection of some kind, in which the spirit or soul will be reunited with a "spiritual body." *How* and *when* this change will take place, the believer in the Incarnation is content to leave in the hands of Him " Who worketh all things after the counsel of His own will."

It is claimed for Jesus, in the Gospel records, that He foretold both His own resurrection and that of mankind, and that His first prediction was actually fulfilled by His rising again the third day.

If we may trust the Gospel records, the real body of Jesus was quickened and raised from the dead, and was seen alive, not once nor twice, but on several occasions, not as an apparition or spiritual phantom, but as a material organism. " Handle Me, and see ; for a spirit hath not flesh and bones, as ye see Me have."

On this point the testimony of St. Peter is very emphatic—

" Him God raised up the third day, and showed Him openly. Not to all the people, but unto witnesses chosen before of God, even to us, who did eat and drink with Him after He rose from the dead " (Acts x. 41, 42).[1]

[1] Cf. 1 Pet. i. 3.

THE SURVIVAL OF MAN 133

There is a tendency at the present time to deny the truth and reality of the resurrection of Jesus, and give it a merely symbolic or metaphorical significance. But this is only a modern recrudescence of an error which made its appearance in the very infancy of the Christian Church. St. Paul refers to it as prevalent in his day. Even then there were some "who concerning the truth have erred, saying that the resurrection is past already, and overthrow the faith of some."[1] But he himself was a firm believer in the literal truth of the resurrection of Jesus. He believed it on the strength of the evidence of eye-witnesses.[2] And when he went forth to his missionary work, the burthen of his preaching was not Jesus only, but "Jesus and the resurrection." In short, it is impossible to eliminate the doctrine of the resurrection of Jesus from the Gospel records and from the body of Christian theology.

But faith in the resurrection of Jesus and in a general resurrection go hand in hand. They stand or fall together. Acceptance of the former involves also acceptance of the latter.

If the resurrection of Jesus must be regarded as an integral and inseparable part of His work and ministry, necessary for the completion of the purpose of the Incarnation; and if we believe that the Incarnation was the manifestation of the

[1] 2 Tim. ii. 18.   [2] 1 Cor. xv. 5, 6.

Logos, as by the Spiritual Philosophy we are bound to do;—then also we need not hesitate to accept the doctrine of a general resurrection, though we may be unable to explain it.

II. THE ARGUMENT FROM EVOLUTION

We have seen what has been accomplished under the continued action of that process of change we call evolution. It has been the production of a self-conscious personality—an individual endowed with marvellous moral and psychical faculties—a spiritual being, capable of entertaining ideas of the loftiest and sublimest character, even the idea of God Himself; conscious of longings and aspirations which nothing short of God Himself can satisfy. Such has been the result achieved under the process of Evolution. Can we imagine it possible, that that process is to be suddenly and completely terminated by the death of the body, and the psychical results so laboriously attained flung away as the mere fiction of a perfervid imagination? Shall we not rather say, that a being which has evolved, or become endowed with, such transcendent faculties must be itself divine, and, therefore, can never die.

Spiritual Philosophy teaches us to believe that the self-conscious soul of man is the offspring of the one Fount of consciousness, which is God, and that henceforth its highest aim should be (to use the words ascribed to Plotinus as his dying exhortation) "to bring the God that is in us into union and communion with the God that is in the All."

When we cast our eyes back over the whole course of vital evolution, from its earliest manifestation in mere reflex action and neurility up to its highest value attained in man, we see that it is, in the main, the history of psychological development, which has found at length its climax in the human race. But the human race is not like a hive of bees, working by instinct for the preservation and welfare of the community. It is of a far higher character, for it consists of separate individuals, each of which has somehow become possessed of free will and self-consciousness, capable of perceiving moral distinctions, and, therefore, severally responsible for the use it makes of the faculties with which it has become endowed. But if the only future life in store for humanity be that of the race in this sublunary sphere, if death spells annihilation for the individual personality,—then the process of vital and psychical evolution would appear to end in a *fiasco*. All the toilsome steps by which the height, so far, has been climbed have only brought us to an *impasse*, and the labour has been in vain. The idea of moral responsibility, which has all along acted as a restraint from evil and an incentive to good, is only an illusion. Nature has played us false. For there is no future sphere of life in which well-doing will be rewarded and evil-doing punished, and in which the sense and conviction of personal responsibility will be justified and realized.

The Place of Death in Evolution

We shall have studied the problem of vital evolution to little effect, if we have not learned that one of the essential laws or canons of vital development is "Life through death. Death the stepping-stone to a higher life."

As Mr. Fiske so admirably puts it: "He who regards man as the consummate fruition of creative Energy, and the chief object of Divine care, is almost irresistibly drawn to the belief that the soul's career is not completed with the present life upon the earth." And again: "The more thoroughly we comprehend that process of evolution by which things have come to be what they are, the more we are likely to feel that to deny the everlasting persistence of the spiritual element in man is to rob the whole process of its meaning."[1]

The whole history of psychical development is characterized by two features: (1) A tendency to freedom, and an ever-growing independence on the

[1] "Destiny of Man," p. 115.

part of the personal ego of material and mechanical limitations and restraints; and (2) the subjugation of the body, with its animal instincts and its fleshly appetites, to the service of the soul.

"Life," says Newman Smith, "has become an extra-physical potency. It is still inwoven with the meshes of fine molecular changes; but it is a life which has escaped from bondage to a purely physical service."[1]

And again: "The existence of some physical substance or material basis for the mind, is not necessary in reason to its actual presence and energy. Even in our modern physics the primary concepts of matter, light and the etherial transmissions of energy, have become so attenuated that they elude the grasp of the common imagination of men. Materiality itself is itself becoming a vanishing point; energy is known to us as a living Will. It were a pure assumption to suppose that spirit must for ever remain tethered to an atom . . . spiritual energy may have other carriage, and more etherial conveyance than the motions of the molecules (of the brain) which it now makes subservient to its uses."[2]

[1] "Place of Death in Evolution," p. 114.
[2] "The Place of Death, etc.," p. 117. I commend the following passage from Dr. McDougall's splendid work on "Body and Mind" to my readers' thoughtful consideration: "Though it is not possible to say just how much of what we call personality is rooted in bodily habit, and how much in psychical dispositions, yet it is open to us to believe that the soul, if it survives the dissolution of the body, carries with it some large part of that which has been gained by intellectual

Two Theories of Cerebral Function in Connection with Thought

The late Prof. W. James, in his Ingersoll Lecture on "Human Immortality," discusses at some length the two theories of cerebral activity in connection with thought. The first is the Production theory held by the materialists, according to which the brain produces thought just as the liver secretes bile. The second is what is called the Transmission theory; because the brain is regarded as the physical and material organ for receiving, registering, and transmitting to the conscious psychè, or soul, ideas or intimations which reach it from without, *i.e.* from the Fount or Source of all consciousness. James also quotes a significant passage from Kant's "*Kritik der reinen Vernunft*," which, he says, presents a close resemblance to the Transmission theory. It runs as follows :—

"The death of the body may indeed be the end of the sensational use of our mind, but only the beginning of the intellectual use. The body and moral effort; and though the acceptance of the view we have suggested as to the essential part played by the body in conditioning the sensory content of consciousness, would make it impossible to suppose that the surviving soul could enjoy the exercise of thought of that kind with which alone we are familiar, yet it is not inconceivable that it might find conditions that would stimulate it to imageless thought (possibly conditions of direct or telepathic communication with other minds), or might find under other conditions (possibly in association with some other bodily organism) a sphere for the application and actualization of the capacities developed in it during its life in the body" (p. 372).

would thus be, not the cause of our thinking, but merely a condition restrictive thereof; and though essential to our sensuous and animal consciousness, it may be regarded as an impeder of our pure spiritual life."

Indeed, to suppose that the brain secretes thought and begets concept and psychical emotion, would, as it seems to me, be as reasonable as to suppose that the telephone or wireless telegraph "receiver" creates the message it transmits. What the "receiver" does is only to collect and record the etheric waves which reach it from a station perhaps hundreds of miles away, and translate them by means of a preconcerted code, into a language easily intelligible. The brain is such a "receiver." It does not create thought, but it transmits thought, and interprets it; the thought itself being, so to speak, a rill of consciousness from the mind of the sender.

Referring to some of "the mysterious phenomena" revealed through psychical research, "it is often hard to see," says Prof. James, "where the sense-organs can come in, and from what sensations, on the production theory, such odd bits of knowledge—as, for instance, the apparition of some one who is now dying hundreds of miles away—are produced. On the transmission theory, they do not have to be 'produced,' they exist ready made in the transcendental world." [1]

[1] "Human Immortality," pp. 53, 54.

The Pauline View

Paul, the Apostle and Christian philosopher, met the difficulty of those who asked, "How are the dead raised, and with what body do they come?" by pointing them to an analogous process in nature—that of the seed sown in the earth: "That which thou sowest, thou sowest not that body which shall be, but a bare grain, it may chance of wheat, or of some other grain: but God giveth it a body even as it pleased Him, and to each seed a body of its own" (1 Cor. xv. 36, 37). So with the resurrection. "There is a natural body, and there is a spiritual body. . . . It is sown a natural body, it is raised a spiritual body" (ver. 44).

The analogy, it is true, like most analogies, does not hold good in all respects. In the case of the seed sown, the outward material form, the *soma-plasm*, perishes, but the *germ-plasm* remains alive, germinates, and produces another plant like the former. But in the death of a human being the body, as an organism, may be entirely destroyed as in cremation, or even become part of another organism. Where and what in this case is the germ-plasm of the new "spiritual body"? Is the spiritual body in any true sense a revivification or development of the old natural body? It does not seem that we can argue from the ordinary method of vital reproduction which goes on in nature, to the resurrection of the human body after the dissolution caused by death; that is, from the natural to the spiritual body. But, because the transition seems to us impossible, shall we dare to say it is so? We know so much of the marvels of Creative Evolution in the past, and so little of the vital energy which underlies them, that such a conclusion would be rash indeed.

But this, at any rate, the analogy is intended to teach us—that the great principle of life through death holds good in the psychical and spiritual sphere as well as in the physical and natural. Surely, when we reflect on our own ignorance and the mighty power of God, it is our wisdom to accept the mystery in humble faith as one which He will solve for us in His own good time and way. The language in which St. Paul confessed his faith in it is that which best becomes us too: "We wait for a Saviour, the Lord Jesus Christ, Who shall fashion anew the body of our humiliation, that it may be conformed to the body of His glory, according to the working whereby He is able to subject all things unto Himself" (Phil. iii. 20, 21).

> "Flower in the crannied wall,
> I pluck you out of the crannies;—
> Hold you here, root and all, in my hand,
> Little flower: but if I could understand
> What you are, root and all, and all in all,
> I should know what God and man is."
>
> Tennyson.

The Argument for Survival from Psychical Research

Beside these two main streams of evidence in favour of the survival of man, there is yet another, which must not be ignored, though at the present time its extent and value cannot be accurately estimated. I refer to the labours of the Psychical Research Society.

"During the last thirty years," says Dr. McDougall, "the Society for Psychical Research has investigated, in a strictly scientific manner, certain obscure phenomena, the occurrence of which had been accepted by the popular mind in all ages and in all countries, but which have been rejected by the official world of modern science as merely superstitious survivals from the dark ages. . . . At the present day, no one undertaking to review the psycho-physical problem can ignore the results of these investigations without laying himself open to the charge of *culpable ignorance* or *unscientific prejudice*. The principal aim of the Society has been to obtain, if possible, empirical evidence that human personality may, and does, survive in some sense or degree the death of the body. A considerable mass of evidence pointing in this direction has been accumulated. Its nature is such that many of those who have devoted attention to the work, and have had a full and first-hand acquaintance with the investigations and their results, have become convinced that survival is a fact." [1]

(1) THE ARGUMENT FOR SURVIVAL AS AFFECTED BY PSYCHICAL RESEARCH

Replying to a question as to the human personality's survival of bodily death, Sir O. Lodge, who is President of the Psychical Research Society, said, "We are certainly nearer such a demonstration, and that which has been in the past a matter of religious faith will become in the future a matter of scientific knowledge. I do not say the proof is crucially complete as yet, but the evidence is so exceedingly strong, that it is only by mental contortion that the cogency can be evaded, and as investigation proceeds every alternative hypothesis becomes more and more strained." And again, in his Presidential Address before the British Association (Sept. 10, 1913), the following passage occurs :—

"The evidence, to my mind, goes to prove that discarnate intelligences, under certain conditions, may interact with us on the material side, thus indirectly coming within our scientific ken; and thus gradually we may hope to attain some understanding of the nature of a larger, perhaps etherial existence, and of the conditions regulating intercourse across the chasm."

That the spirits of men have power to make

[1] "Body and Mind," p. 347.

themselves visible to friend or relative at or about the time of death, or even at some critical juncture of their lives, does not, I think, admit of doubt.[1]

"Unless we reject all testimony," says Mr. W. F. Barrett, "or attribute the numerous cases investigated to some illusion, there can be no doubt that a distant person can, by his directed thought or by dream, create a phantom of himself in the mind of a distant percipient."[2]

"I will see thee again at Philippi," said the ghost of the murdered Cæsar, to his heartless quondam friend, as he sat in his tent on the eve of the battle of Pharsalia.[3]

---

[1] For thus introducing the subject of psychical research in his Presidential Address, Sir Ray Lankester has taken Sir O. Lodge severely to task. He charges him with "the intrusion of suppositions and beliefs as to ghostly existences, unaccompanied by the smallest attempt at demonstration, into the proceedings of an Association for the Advancement of Science." But surely this is hardly fair criticism. For, though Sir Oliver did not produce a real ghost on the platform, he distinctly asserted that the beliefs and possibilities for which he contends are founded on facts and phenomena sufficient to convince him and many others of their truth and reality. Will Sir Ray deny that there are facts and phenomena displayed through psychic activity with which at present we are very imperfectly acquainted? If not, then, the study and investigation of them has as much right to be considered a branch of science as physics or physiology. The domain of science has been vastly increased since the time when even the British Association was founded. (See "Science from an Easy Chair," Sept. 30, 1913.)

[2] "Psychical Research." Mr. Barrett gives the following amongst other instances: "On one occasion the phantom of Mr. Beard was seen and recognized by two persons in the room simultaneously, who were unaware of the fact that Mr. Beard, some miles away, was then trying by an effort of will to appear to them."

[3] *Julius Cæsar*, act iv. sc. 3.

Some of my readers, perhaps, may be able to testify to the reality of such apparitions at the time of death by instances which have come within their own experience.[1] But whether or not, the instances recorded are too numerous and well-authenticated to be called in question. Over two hundred such cases have already been investigated by the Psychical Research Society, and found to rest on unimpeachable evidence. Such apparitions or phantasms are called wraiths, and are usually explained as due to telepathic influence exerted by the spirit of the dead or dying person. Mr. Myers, however, preferred to regard them as examples of the *excursive* power and action of the departing spirit.

The value of such evidence as this must not be underrated, though at the same time, we must admit it falls far short of proving the possibility

[1] I cannot forbear to mention the following instance of a very remarkable and interesting instance of psychic manifestation which occurred to a dear lady friend and relative of mine so recently as November 13, 1913,—She was watching by the bed-side of her husband, who was at the time at the point of death. She relates how between his final gasps for breath, when his soul was just about to quit its earthly tenement, she suddenly and distinctly heard sweet strains of vocal music, not in the room, but proceeding as it were from a choir of minstrels high up in heaven above, and singing a hymn, one line or refrain of which was quite clearly audible:

"Thou blest Rock of Ages, I'm hiding in Thee."

Another gasp, and the spirit had fled, and the music died away as suddenly as it had come. Need I say that my friend was deeply impressed and comforted by the occurrence? for she regarded it as a Heaven-sent intimation from her husband that all was well with his soul.

146   THE SPIRITUAL PHILOSOPHY

and actuality of communication between the dead and the living. The Myers' test,[1] upon which great hopes had been placed, certainly proved a complete failure, greatly to the disappointment of those who had charge of it. And the evidence of the "*survival*" afforded by automatic writing and cross-correspondences seems to me to be too vague and speculative to be worth much. Dr. McDougall, however, thinks it may prove valuable.

(2) PSYCHICAL RESEARCH IN RELATION TO THE SPIRITUAL PHILOSOPHY

But whether or not the veridical results of psychical research up to the present time afford additional evidence of the survival of man, they have a distinct value of their own in relation to the Spiritual Philosophy.

For the facts and phenomena disclosed are of such a nature as to be quite irreconcilable with any theory of mechanistic materialism. If they

---

[1] The following is a brief account of the so-called Myers' test. The script was sent by Mr. Myers to Sir O. Lodge in January, 1891, in a sealed envelope, which was not to be opened until after Mr. Myers' death. Mrs. Verrall, who developed the faculty of automatic writing soon after Mr. Myers' decease, professed to have received intimations of what were the contents of the sealed envelope. On Tuesday, December 13, 1904, after Mr. Myers' death, the letter was opened and read, when it was found that there was no resemblance between its actual contents and Mrs. Verrall's automatic script. The experiment completely failed, and, adds Sir O. Lodge "the failure is disappointing."
—"The Survival of Man," p. 123.

are real and true, then the agency which causes them must be of a spiritual character.[1]

Already, great and valuable additions have been made to our knowledge of the constitution, the content, and the capacity of the human personality, especially in the sub-conscious or sub-liminal region. I refer more particularly to the remarkable phenomena of telepathy and will-power, to the astonishing " awareness of the passage of time, and the supernormal faculty for making difficult arithmetical calculations, displayed by persons in the hypnotic state."

Physiology has long been regarded as a legitimate branch of science. Why should not psychology be similarly regarded? If the true line of vital development is psychical rather than physical, then the study of human psychology should occupy a position of paramount importance in relation to the process of vital evolution and the survival of man.

---

[1] " This, then, is the principal importance I attach to the results hitherto achieved by psychical research; namely, I regard it as having established the occurrence of phenomena which cannot be reconciled with the mechanistic scheme of things."—Dr. McDougall's "Body and Mind," p. 350.

CHAPTER XIV

RECAPITULATION AND CONCLUSION

LET me now, in conclusion, recapitulate and summarize the principal points I have endeavoured to establish.

Starting from the highest point attained in Prof. Romanes' Diagram of Mental Evolution in Animals, my aim has been to follow the course of psychic evolution in man, through its successive stages of religious, moral, and spiritual consciousness.

Two factors have been engaged in this process.

(*a*) The Divine Energy of the Transcendent Deity, manifested in the universe through the creative Logos and the enforming life-giving Spirit of Wisdom.

(*b*) The activity of the free, self-conscious personality of man displayed in percept, apperception, and concept.

By the presence and interaction of these two factors the process has been carried forward until the climax of psychical evolution has been attained in the soul of man, a spiritual entity capable of knowing God, of bearing and reflecting the image of God, and so fitted to enter into loving fellowship and communion with Him.

Summary and Conclusion

Science, religion, philosophy, are three very real factors in human thought and human progress, not one of which we can afford to ignore. Science is not philosophy, neither is religion. Yet a philosophy we must have of some kind. For the *rôle* of philosophy is like that of the weaver—to gather up the scattered and tangled threads of our experience, and patiently weave them into the beautiful garment of Truth.

The main problem which has engaged our attention is the right interpretation of Evolution, its cause, its method, its products, and end. Science, if it means no more than the investigation of the laws and phenomena of the physical and material universe, is incapable of giving the solution we seek, because, beside the physical and material, there are psychical and spiritual phenomena, equally real, with which natural science is incompetent to deal. Such are the intellectual and moral faculties of the mind, the religious instincts, yearnings, and aspirations of the soul. Are we to ignore them, or, like the Materialists, rest satisfied when we have called them "epiphenomena," which accompany nervous and cerebral action? We cannot do so, because reason assures us that these things are of a higher order than matter and motion, and, as we have said again and again, the nature and cause of Evolution must be gathered from the highest values it has been able to produce. And if amongst those highest values we are able to point to the personal self-conscious soul of man, then the cause, which underlies and energizes the process, cannot be less than a Personal Self-conscious Spirit.

Thankfully, indeed, we welcome all the light that Science can throw on the problem of life, all the additions she can make to our stock of knowledge of the universe; but at the same time, we cannot shut our eyes to the fact that there are phases and departments of vital activity which do not fall within the scope of the scientist or natural philosopher to analyze; and there are human needs which Science can never meet.

What, for example, can Science do to lighten the load of sin and suffering? What for the training and development of moral character? What for the satisfaction of the religious yearnings and aspirations of the soul? These are real, every-day wants—no mere epiphenomena—and Science alone can never satisfy them.

We had begun to say, "Materialism is dead." We fondly imagined that the automaton theory had been for ever relegated to the limbo of exploded and forgotten fallacies. But, lo! it has appeared once more, like a grim spectre, seeking to lay the icy finger of death on the best hopes and aspirations of mankind.

Percept and apperception, concept and response (conation),—these are successive steps, which indicate the method and mark the upward progress of psychical development. Starting from the lowest forms of animal life, where little more than mere reflex action, without sense-organs, was observable, we have been carried along by successive increments of psychic consciousness, till we have reached that *chef-d'œuvre* of the evolutionary process, the self-conscious personal Soul of man.

But why is Man here at all? For what purpose all this elaborate age-long preparation? Was it only that he might spend a few years of joy or sorrow on the earth, and then be swallowed up in the abyss of death and oblivion? that he might pass his little day of life in pride and self-pleasing, regarding the great drama of Evolution as though it were some spectacular show, some variety entertainment, in which his part is only that of a passive spectator?

No! Reason and revelation alike forbid us to take so mean a view of the end and object of Evolution.

"If man be the crown of Nature's vital processes, so far as his physical constitution is concerned, he bears in his psychical organization marks that he is meant for higher things than can be attained within the narrow margin of existence permitted to him here."[1] As God is the Source, so is He the only worthy End and Object of the spirit of man. And, to quote again from the same author: "To be brought in ever closer touch with the Father of Lights, to develop and multiply those intimate relationships with Him which are the soul's life-breath . . . to come to know Him and to love Him, and to love what He loves; to make His will our will, and find our meat and drink in the doing of that will: this is to be spiritually minded. And it is this which not only gives the richest and fullest sense of life in every way, but is the only assurance we can possibly have of a blessed immortality in the world to come."[2]

What, then, shall our Philosophy be? Shall it be that Mechanistic Materialism, which ignores the existence of God, and slays the souls of men; which denies them freedom and immortality, and regards the Christian's hope as the illusion of a perfervid imagination? Or shall it be that animistic Spiritual Philosophy, which is based on our varied experience and the reasonable inferences drawn therefrom; which takes into account "all that is given," and interprets Evolution, not as a melancholy, meaningless procession, to end only in death and annihilation, but as the method adopted by

[1] "Ascent through Christ," p. 440.
[2] *Ibid.*, pp. 397, 398.

RECAPITULATION AND CONCLUSION

the Transcendent Deity for His self-manifestation, and opens out for mankind the vista of illimitable progress towards perfection, when the creature, which was "made subject to vanity," shall be delivered from the bondage of corruption into "the glorious liberty of the sons of God"? Which shall it be? Time alone can show.

"Oh, send out Thy light and Thy truth, that they may lead me, and bring me to Thy holy hill and to Thy dwelling."

> "To God again the enfranchised soul must tend.
> He is her Home, her Author, and her End.
> No death is hers when earthly eyes grow dim:
> Star-like she soars, and God-like melts in Him."

Such, then, is that system of Spiritual Philosophy, an outline of which—and nothing more—I have endeavoured to give in the foregoing pages. I am deeply conscious of some at least of the many faults and imperfections which may be found in my handling of so great a subject; nor can I expect to carry along with me the assent of all my Readers to the propositions I have endeavoured to establish. But there is one favour I have to ask, which I hope will not be denied me. It is, a patient and unbiassed hearing from those who, like myself, are humble and earnest seekers after Truth.

FINIS

APPENDIX

NOTE A

GOOD AND EVIL

(1) THE following is a digest of some of the theories which have been held and expressed by various writers on the problem of good and evil, extracted from Dr. Inge's "Christian Mysticism":—

Gregory of Nyssa.—"Evil has no substance. There is nothing which falls outside of the Divine nature, except moral evil alone. And this we may say, paradoxically, has its being in not-being. For the genesis of moral evil is simply the privation of being. That which, properly speaking, exists is the nature of the good."

Eregina.—"Nothing is opposed to God." "Every visible and invisible creature is a theophany or appearance of God." "There may be Goodness without Being, but not Being without Goodness; for evil is the negation of Being."

Plotinus.—In the system of this philosopher evil has merely a negative existence, and matter, as the indigence of all positive qualities, that is, of all good, is identified with evil ("Enn.," II. lib. iv. sec. 16).

Only the knowledge of evil is attributable to the Deity. Its actual experience by us is due to a voluntary determination of the individual consciousness towards the material or sensuous plane ("Enn.," III. lib. ii. sec. 7).

Dionysius and the system of Hierotheus.—Evil is that which is nowhere, nohow, and no thing. It is simply a kind of accident arising from "disorderly and inharmonious motion." It is the good gone wrong. And God Himself sees evil as good.

Augustine speaks of evil as simple privation of good. It is like the splash of dark colour which gives relief to the picture.

Tauler.—"The essence of sin, according to Tauler, is self-assertion or self-will, and consequent separation from God. Sensuality and pride, the two chief manifestations of self-will, have invaded the whole of our nature. Pride is a sin of the spirit, and the poison has invaded 'even the ground —the created ground,' that is, as the unity of all the faculties. . . . Tauler seems to believe that under one aspect 'the created ground' is the transparent medium of the Divine Light, but in this sense it is only potentially the light of our whole body. He will not allow the sinless *apex mentis* to be identified with the personality. Separation from God is the source of all misery. Herein lies the pain of Hell. The human soul can never cease to yearn and thirst after God; 'and the greatest pain of the lost' is that this longing can never be satisfied."—"Christian Mysticism," p. 185.

Dr. Laurie ("Synthetica").—The whole treatise is highly metaphysical, and turns mainly on the difference between affirmation and negation. Evil is defined as the negative of good, and at the same time, the condition of the good. " Without evil there could be no living movement of personality, no real achievement or development. How evil is to be conceived from the point of view of the Absolute, is, from the nature of the case, indeterminable. God certainly is the Source of evil, as of everything; but this does not mean that He created it."

For my part, I am unable to subscribe to the "negation" or "privative" theory of evil. And that for the following reasons:—

The very term " good " implies the existence of something which is not only "not good," but "bad." Should we know the "good" were it not for the antithesis between it and something which is opposed to it? If evil were only the negative of good, and had no positive character or real existence, what then becomes of "choice"?

In that case there would be no alternatives to choose between, for there would be nothing left but "the good" and a negation which we can neither define nor grasp. If there be no radical and positive difference between good and evil, then how are we to account for "the percept of ethical distinctions," and, consequently, for the concept of moral character and conduct?

But we may go even further than this. The whole process of Evolution, vital and psychical, is based on the antagonism between "good" and "evil." "The struggle for existence," and "the survival of the fittest," are not these the recognized canons of evolutionary progress? But were there no antagonistic forces or principles, there need be, and there could be, no "struggle," and, therefore, no "survival of the fittest."

It is useless, as Kant says, to bewilder ourselves with vain attempts to account for the origin of evil in the past, or to forecast its fate in the future. Surely it is enough for us to recognize its reality in the present, and that, for the individual and the race, further progress can only be secured by entering into the strife, and "overcoming the evil by the good."

NOTE B

ADDITIONAL NOTE ON CONSCIOUSNESS

I AM aware, of course, of the hypotheses whereby the supporters of Materialism seek to explain the facts of consciousness and conscious action, namely, as *Epiphenomenalism and Psycho-physical Parallelism.*

"It was Huxley," says Dr. McDougall, who "invented the first of these terms. He suggested that the stream of consciousness should be called epiphenomenal, or the epiphenomenon of the brain process. . . . The consciousness of any organism is caused by some immediately preceding physical or chemical change occurring in the brain of that organism."—"Body and Mind," p. 127.

The second term, "Psycho-physical Parallelism," is used to denote that physical (cerebral) and psychical processes are equally real, but that there is no interaction between them. They do not influence one another, and the relation between them is that of concomitance only. They resemble two railway trains running side by side, but quite independently of each other.

But both these hypotheses are open to serious objections. If consciousness be due to purely material and mechanical causes acting according to rigid physical laws, then consciousness, if it could emerge at all, must always be in subjection to those laws. We reduce all vital, mental, and psychical activity to a condition of *determinism,* in which freedom and reasoned action by the self-conscious personality is for ever impossible, and man becomes a mere automaton. But does our experience of human life and

APPENDIX 159

conscious activity support such a view? Under such a system there is no room for a free self-conscious Ego, nor yet for religious or moral consciousness. The very distinction between good and evil is done away. The murderer is no more to blame than the most self-denying philanthropist, for neither has any choice in his actions. They both act in strict accordance to the stern law of mechanical necessity, which it is impossible for them to resist. Does it not seem more likely that consciousness and mental activity are not the result of molecular changes in the brain, but that these latter, on the contrary, are due to the former? And, if this be so, would it not be truer to say that cerebral changes are the epiphenomena of psychic consciousness than that psychic manifestations, such as thought, free will, and choice, are the epiphenomena resulting from cerebral change? Or, to put it still more briefly, that it is the mind which has produced brain, and not brain the mind? And this, indeed, is what is asserted in the identity hypothesis of psychical monism.

According to this view, says Prof. McDougall (p. 133), all causal efficiency is due to the psychical series, and matter and all its processes are but as it were the shadows thrown by thought on the blank sheet of our experience. It is thus the converse of epiphenomenalism.

There is yet another argument against the doctrine of psycho-physical parallelism, which is of considerable weight in my mind. It is the following:—

Consciousness, we have seen, has been continuous throughout the whole course of psychic evolution. And the successive movements are united by the means of a self-conscious personality, which assimilates and enriches itself by each new concept as it arises. But, according to the doctrine of psycho-physical parallelism, physical and psychical processes simply accompany one another. There is no causal connection or interaction between them. Each act of consciousness is separate and distinct.

It arises like a phosphorescent glow. It exists for a moment, and then passes away as though it had never been. Where in this case is the nexus to bind the successive acts and processes of consciousness together, to unify and integrate them as increments in the progress of psychical development?

But, after all, are not these discussions as to the respective claims of matter or mind for causal priority in vital evolution somewhat beside the mark? Do they not betoken a misconception of the real problem before us? The solution of that problem, as it seems to me, is not to be found in the antagonism of matter and mind, of brain and consciousness, but rather in their synthesis and co-ordination as forms of energy and co-operant factors in working out the great purposes of Evolution—the manifestation of the Infinite in the finite, and the approximation of the creature to the Creator, of the human to the Divine.

NOTE C

SIN

WHAT is sin? This is a question of vast importance, owing to its universal prevalence and its baneful effects. And what is both a remarkable and significant fact, is that the root or origin of the word, in the Teutonic and Scandinavian families of language, is so ancient as to be beyond the reach of recovery. All that the etymologists can do is to suggest a connection between the word in its earliest forms and the Latin *sous*,[1] signifying *hurtful, noxious*,[2] *guilty*.

But if the English word *sin* (A.S. *syn*; Ger. *sünde*) refuses to disclose the radical idea which underlies it, perhaps the synonyms for *sin* in other ancient languages may help us.

In the Hebrew, for instance, the earliest word used to denote sin is *hātā*. Of this word Robertson Smith writes: "The fundamental meaning of the Hebrew word *hātā*, to sin, is to be at fault, and in Hebrew, as in Arabic, the active form has the sense of missing the mark (Judg. xx. 16) or other object aimed at. The

---

[1] Probably connected with the Greek σίντης, adj. = *tearing, ravenous*; subst. = *a poisonous snake, a fox, a thief*; and this, again, with σίνομαι = *to plunder, spoil, wound*.

[2] *Sonticus morbus* is a noxious disease. The similarity in sound between the Latin *sonticus* and the German *sundig* is certainly striking. It is remarkable that in the Gothic the idea of *sin* is represented by quite a different word, *fra-vaurhts* = unrighteousness, the opposite of *ns-vaurhts* = righteousness.

162 THE SPIRITUAL PHILOSOPHY

notion of sin, therefore, is that of blunder or dereliction, and the word is associated with others that indicate error, folly, or want of skill and insight (1 Sam. xxvi. 21). ... In two respects, then, the Hebrew idea of sin, in its earlier stages, is quite distinct from that which we attach to the word. In the first place, it is not necessarily thought of as an offence against God, but includes any act that puts a man in the wrong with those who have power to make him rue it (2 Kings xviii. 14; 1 Sam. xx. 1). In the second place, the notion of sin has no necessary reference to the conscience of the sinner; it does not necessarily involve moral guilt, but only, so to speak, forensic liability.[1]

Similarly, the Greek word used to denote sin, *hamartia*, does not appear at first to have possessed any moral significance, but merely to have conveyed the idea of missing the mark, either through mistake or want of skill.

Fra-vaurhts is the Gothic synonym for *sin*.

Although the Gothic belongs to the same family of languages as the Anglo-Saxon, it is somewhat remarkable that the word commonly used to denote "sin" in the other branches of the family is not found here also, as we should naturally have expected.

Instead of a word of that type, we find one entirely different, namely, *fra-vaurhts*,[2] which really signifies mis-working or counter-working. So if the Gothic has lost the word for sin which is common to the other

---

[1] "Prophets of Israel," pp. 102 f.

[2] The Gothic prefix *fra-* corresponds to the A.S. and English *for-* as in *for-bid, for-give, for-sake*, etc., and often gives the idea of privation, deterioration, or even destruction. In A.S. we have the same verb as that which in the Gothic yielded *fra-vaurhts* = sin, namely, *for-wyrcan*, signifying to mis-work, to oppose, to corrupt, to spoil. There is also a verbal substantive *for-worht*, corresponding exactly in form with Gothic *fra-vaurhts*, but denoting, not sin, but the sinner himself—one condemned, a malefactor.

branches of the Teutonic family, it has, at any rate, retained one which embodies a very definite and instructive idea of the nature of sin, namely, as something which produces undoing, deterioration, and destruction.

The word commonly used in the Latin to denote sin is *peccatum*, whence comes our word *peccadillo* = a little sin. If the supposition be correct, that the word *pecco* is only a contracted form of *pecudico* = to act like a sheep, which is apt to wander away and get lost in the wilderness,[1] we see that here again, in the first instance, the word implied no moral stigma or consciousness of guilt.

In all the above cases it would appear that the primitive idea or concept of sin was merely that of failure or mistake, which might, indeed, entail serious consequences, but which implied no moral delinquency or guiltiness.

It was, then, the concept of moral law that gave to all these synonyms of sin, *fra-vaurhts, hamartia, peccatum*, their moral significance. Where there is no law there can be no transgression, no disobedience, and therefore no sin.[2] For sin is the transgression of law; and the higher the law, that is, the clearer the manifestation of moral goodness, the greater is the sin of disobedience and failure to respond to it.[3]

[1] Cp. Ps. cxix. 176, "I have gone astray like a sheep that is lost." "We have erred and strayed from Thy ways like lost sheep" ("General Confession").

[2] St. Paul was very clear and emphatic on this point. "I had not known lust," he says, "except the Law had said, Thou shalt not covet." "I was alive once without the Law, but when the Law came, sin revived, and I died." He draws an awful picture of the gross corruption of Roman society in his day. And one of the foulest sins which stained it was that of unnatural lust and impurity, in short, it was the sin of disobedience to the laws of nature (Rom. i. 26, 27).

[3] This is well brought out by St. Paul in Rom. vii. 22-24. It was the antagonism and strife between the two laws—the lower, that of animal propensity, and the higher, that of God—realized in his own experience, which caused him such grave apprehension as to the result.

"I delight in the law of God after the inward man. But I see another law in my members, warring against the law of my mind, and bringing me into captivity to the law of sin, which is in my members. O wretched man that I am! Who shall deliver me from the body of this death?"

INDEX

Anima, 2
Animistic, 152
Antithesis, 60-62
Apperception, 34
—— Kant, Leibniz, and Reid on, 35
Askwith, Dr., on sin, 109
Atoms, composite bodies, 7
—— "with souls," 8
Atonement, doctrine of, 109
—— substitutional view, 110

Barrett, W. T., 144
Beauty, concrete and abstract, 50
—— distinct from utility, 25
—— idea of, 50
—— Plato on, 51
Bergson's theory of life, 18
—— on "Life and Consciousness," 39 note
Brain, 5, 158
Brotherhood of Man, 91, 119

Caldecott, Dr., 122 note
Cerebral activity, 138, 139
Christian theology, 16
Christus, Pastor, Se Hælend, Consolator, 93
—— Redemptor, 94
—— Rex, 95
—— Intercessor, 96
Claims of Jesus, 80
—— made by His disciples, 81
—— —— by Himself, 83

Conation, 37
Concepts, 36
—— Prof. James on, 36 note
Congruity, mark of, 63
Consciousness, evolution of, 30, 67, Note B
—— moral, 55 ff., 65
—— of Jesus, 98
—— Prof. Wundt on, 67
—— religious, 53
—— self, 40, 41
—— spiritual, 77
Creative Evolution, 1
—— as displaying intelligence, purpose, and directivity, 25, 26

Darwin, Charles, on the Religious Concept, 53
Design, 24
Diagrams—
  No. 1: Romanes', 18, 24
  No. 2: Psychical development in man, 28
Directivity, 50
Duty, 71

Ego and Personality, 41
Electrons, 8, 9
Energy, 10, 38
—— category of, 12
—— Monistic, 12
Environment, the new, 104
Epiphenomenalism, 158, Note B
—— Dr. McDougall on, 159

Ether, 8, 52
Ethical distinctions, 55
Evolution, Creative, 1
—— further progress of, 20, 21
—— mental, in animals, 23-27
—— place of death in, 136, 137
—————— Dr. McDougall, 137 note

Fatherhood of God, 117
Fiske, Dr., persistence of the soul, 136
Free-will, 41

Good and evil, problem of, 56, 113
—— —— various theories, 156
—— Principal Tulloch on, 56 note
—— Prof. W. James, 58
—— Prof. Wundt, 57
—— view of Kant, 56
Ghost theory as origin of religious concept, 52
Gustave le Bon, 9

Hammurabi, Code of, 70
Hokmah, 17
Holy Spirit, the—
—— in Old Testament, 125
—— in New Testament, 126
—— concepts arising therefrom, 127, 128

Idea of God, 37
—— Wundt on, 43; Diag. 2, Col. III.
—— of the Good, 66
Ideal moral character, 85, 86
Immortality, 131
—— Kant, 138
—— Prof. James, Ingersoll Lecture on, 138
—— Dr. McDougall, 137 note
—— Dr. Momerie, 130

Incarnation, 78
—— A priori view, 78
—— probable, 79
Infinite, the idea of the, 51
Instinct, religious, 48, 53

Law universal, 69, 73
—— Physical and Natural, 5, 69
—— Moral and Social, 70, 71
—— —— —— Spiritual, 74
Logos, the, 27, 29
Love the Norm of the highest life, 107, 114

Materialism, 27
Materialist's solution, 5, 150, 152
Matter, 7
—— Mendeleeff's view of, 9
Memory, 25
Mental Evolution, 23
Metabolism, 11
Miracles, 98, 102
Moral law, 69, 74
Myers, 145
—— test, 146 and note

Noumena, 35, 48

Panergete, the, 13
Paraclete, the, 13
Penalty, 74
Percepts, 32, 33
Personality, 116
Phenomena, 35, 47
Phronema, the, 44
Physiological psychology, 4
Picture of Jesus, 101-103
Pluralism, 122 ff.
Pragmatism, 55
Prime Cause, 12, 50
Production theory, 138
Psychè, 2
—— in Greek philosophy, 3

INDEX

Psychical research, 142-147
Psychology, 2
Psycho-physical Parallelism, 158

Realities, ultimate physical, 10
Reality, 37; Diag. 2, Col. III.
Response, 114
Responsibility, Diag. 2, Col. III.
Resurrection, 101, 133, 144 ff.

Selbst-heit, 40
Self-consciousness, Diag. 2, Col. III., 35
Sin, 72 and Note C
—— Rev. C. Moxon on, 73 *note*
—— synonyms of, 162
Soul, birth of the, 36, 42
Spiritualistic theories, 120
—— —— —— monistic, 122 ff.
—— —— —— pluralistic, 121
Survival of man, 131

Survival of man, argument from Faith, 132
—— —— from Evolution, 134
—— Dr. McDougall on, 137 *note*
—— Newman Smith on, 137

Tauler, 156
Transcendence, 15, 16
Transmission theory, 139
Trinity, the, 16, 17 *note*

Williams, Dr. H. S., on the Electron, 8 *note* 1
Wraiths, 145
Wundt, Prof., on the Ego and Personality, 42
—— on the Creative World-will, 43 *note*
—— on the ideal moral character, 86

THE END

www.ingramcontent.com/pod-product-compliance
Lightning Source LLC
Chambersburg PA
CBHW051100160426
43193CB00010B/1262